COCKE COUNTY

TENNESSEE

COCKE COUNTY

TENNESSEE

PAGES FROM THE PAST

EDWARD R. WALKER III
COCKE COUNTY HISTORIAN

THE
History
PRESS

Published by The History Press
Charleston, SC 29403
www.historypress.net

First published 2007

ISBN 9781540229229

Library of Congress Cataloging-in-Publication Data

Walker, Edward R., 1950-
Cocke County, Tennessee : pages from the past / Edward R. Walker, III.
p. cm.
Based on the author's column Page from the past which appeared in the Newport plain talk from 1996 to 2001.
ISBN-13: 9781540229229 1. Cocke County (Tenn.)--History--Anecdotes.
2. Cocke County (Tenn.)--Social life and customs--Anecdotes. 3.
Cocke County (Tenn.)--Biography--Anecdotes. 4. Cocke County (Tenn.)--History,
Local--Anecdotes. 5. Newport (Tenn.)--History--Anecdotes. 6. Newport (Tenn.)--Social
life and customs--Anecdotes. 7. Newport (Tenn.)--Biography--Anecdotes. I. Title.
F443.C6W35 2007
976.8'89505--dc22
2007038772

For Cindy and Claire: You have brightened the pages of my history.

Contents

Acknowledgements

M y wonderful family has been tolerant of me when I have been involved in my "historical pursuits," even the times when they have actually accompanied me in the heat or the cold to an old cemetery or an old house. Can I ever repay you?

I also wish to thank David Popiel, editor of the *Newport Plain Talk*, who provided me the opportunity to write these articles, and also to the various members of the staff who have been available when needed— Dion Dykes, Jeff Manes, Duay O'Neil, Penny Webb, Sandy Proffitt and Angela Hull.

Stokely Memorial Library has provided so much of the resource material for my articles, and its staff (Polly, Meschelyn, Pauline and Marie) has always been helpful.

Lastly, a word of appreciation to all of my readers and friends: your suggestions, assistance, compliments and words of encouragement have meant so much to me.

Introduction

Why My Interest in History?

O ne must be predisposed for such an interest, much like one could be predisposed in other areas such as horticulture, music, athletics, art, charisma or diplomacy.

The beginnings of my interest in history lay with my grandparents. My paternal grandmother often amused and pacified me when I was a youngster with stories of days past, particularly those of her childhood and youth. My maternal grandmother, though not a storyteller, had a passion for antiques. Both ladies evinced a link between the present and the past. I can also now recognize that both of my grandfathers contributed to my historical interests.

I always seemed drawn to anything that seemed historical—old houses, antiques, cemeteries, the elderly—and the stories that each had to tell. In my freshman high school year, a biology teacher had her class bring in their family trees in conjunction with a unit on genetics. Though I was not in that class, I began to research my genealogy so I could have that assignment completed if ever assigned. I never received such an assignment, but I have been "climbing family trees" ever since, and even though only a small branch of my family tree is in Cocke County, my interest in local history seems to have evolved simultaneously.

Cocke County is unique. Established in 1797, it is one of the older counties in the state, but for many years so few individuals were interested in its history. Was it because life was so hard here and living in the present took precedence over preserving the past? Might it be our limited exposure to higher education? Could it have been that with the burning of our courthouse in 1876, the citizens felt that all of our history had been destroyed? With their records intact, both neighboring parent counties of Jefferson and Greene regard their histories with pride.

Fortunately, there have been a few Cocke Countians who had an interest in preserving its history. The first was William J. McSween (1848–1914), a local attorney who penned a series of articles entitled "Early Recollections of Newport and Cocke County," which first appeared in a local newspaper in 1903. McSween had the advantage of knowing many persons who had firsthand knowledge of the county's earliest days, as well as the ability to put all that he had learned on paper.

Mrs. Cora Massey Mims (1868–1956) was an individual who from her young days was looking at the community, its families and its churches from a historical perspective. She, too, put much of her memory and research into newspaper articles.

Mrs. Ruth Webb O'Dell (1886–1956) made an invaluable contribution in preserving the county's history with her book *Over The Misty Blue Hills*, which was published in 1951. She never identified what inspired her to undertake this mammoth task, which consumed much of her time for years, but she was a woman ahead of her time: the first female school superintendent in Cocke County (1920), first female president of the East Tennessee Education Association (1923) and first female elected to a second term in the Tennessee General Assembly (1938). Mrs. O'Dell's book did not receive wide local acclaim at first, but as the years passed, more citizens began to realize what a service "Lady Ruth" had rendered the county.

In 1965, Miss Mary Rowe Ruble (1895–1982) was appointed Cocke County historian, to succeed Wilma Dykeman Stokely. In 1966, the new Stokely Memorial Library opened, and Miss Ruble started a genealogy collection with Mrs. O'Dell's book and a one-drawer filing cabinet. Miss Ruble's vision has grown into a separate room with hundreds of volumes, rolls of microfilm, computers and six cabinets crammed with family information, used by visitors from all across the United States. It was Miss Ruble who encouraged Nancy O'Neil and Duay O'Neil to begin a catalogue of all of Cocke County's cemeteries, which they published in 1972 in three volumes titled *Sacred to the Memory*. Miss Ruble, too, encouraged my interest in local history, and in 1976, when she was no longer able to be county historian, she nominated me to succeed her.

Why My Interest in History?

The bicentennial year was 1976, and the next year the television miniseries *Roots* aired; both events inspired Americans to take more interest in their heritage. Such was the case in Cocke County. A local museum was established, civic clubs have undertaken historical projects, several books relating to local history and genealogy have been published, there is interest in membership in patriotic organizations and items on local history in the local newspaper are always popular.

From 1996 until 2001, I wrote a weekly column for the *Newport Plain Talk* titled "Page from the Past." Beginning with only a few ideas, I noticed that as the weeks passed, new topics were forever popping up. Readers would often make a suggestion based upon an old picture, a newspaper clipping, a memory or a question. Doing this series was quite enjoyable and was a learning experience for me. When I was no longer doing the weekly articles, I occasionally submitted articles for the paper's biannual edition, *A Place Called Home*.

This work, *Cocke County, Tennessee: Pages from the Past*, is taken from these articles. It is published with the intention to preserve the history of Cocke County with the hope that it could inspire others to do likewise.

The Story of Newport's Cross

I have been asked several times about the white cross on the cliff in the eastern end of town, so I feel that it might be necessary to repeat its true story. I am drawing on the information from Mrs. W.O. Mims and Herman Knowles, who both had firsthand knowledge of the cross's origin.

The first cross on that spot was placed there temporarily in 1885 by J.W.P. Massey, a brother of Mrs. Mims. She wrote the story of this cross in the *Plain Talk and Tribune* in 1947. Her article was reprinted in "Traces of the Past," a series of historical articles published in the *Newport Plain Talk* in 1975 and 1976 as part of America's bicentennial. This is what Mrs. Mims wrote:

> I have before me a copy of the Newport Times, *Oct. 3, 1900. It gives a vivid account of the accident. The work of raising the railway grade was then in progress and freight trains pulled up Main Street at a slow rate giving boys an opportunity to swing on and get transportation to Eastport to see the Saturday afternoon ball game. Little Vassar Brown tried to keep up with the crowd. He was only 12 years old and was killed just in front of the Alex Ragan home. His father was in Alabama and did not reach Newport until the following day. He* [Vassar] *was buried from the Southern Methodist Church on Monday by Rev. J.W. Browning. The Brown home was on Woodlawn, quite near that of Robert Knowles, which accounts for the affection he felt for the little boy. Vassar was an attractive child.*

A cross on this promontory has towered over Newport for over one hundred years. *Courtesy of Claire Walker.*

In the *Knoxville Journal* of November 14, 1980, Herman Knowles recounted his memory of the cross's origin:

> *There used to be a baseball diamond up around Frog Pond and boys used to swing a freight train from Stokely Brothers Factory...He said that a family named Brown moved to Newport around the turn of the century so Mr. Brown could build houses. Knowles said Brown built some of our finest homes, including the Bruce Robinson home and the Ben Jones' place.*
>
> *The Browns had a 15-year-old son, Vassar Brown, who became a close friend of Bob Knowles—the town's only policeman for many years.*
>
> *"My father and the boy were taking a freight up to the ball park when the boy fell from the train. The train ran over him and killed him."*
>
> *"My father was so attached to this boy that he wanted to build a memorial to him."*
>
> *The younger Knowles said his father, with the help of friends, selected a site where the cross would be visible and climbed up the 70-foot-high bluff, dragging the pieces of poplar wood up with a rope.*
>
> *Herman Knowles says he doesn't know exactly when this happened, but he knows the cross was put up shortly before he was born in 1901.*

Robert Knowles erected the first cross in memory of Vassar Brown. *Courtesy of Vanda L. Knowles.*

The account of the accident was printed in the *Newport Plain Talk* of September 29, 1900, and was reprinted in Montgomery's *Vindication* on October 10, 1900:

A Sad Accident
Little Vassar Brown Cut in Two by a Train

About 2 o'clock today several boys started to the ball grounds in the east end of town. When about opposite the residence of Mr. A. Ragan, Vassar Brown, the son of Contractor O.W. Brown of Newport climbed up on a passing train and walked between the cars to the opposite side. In passing between the cars he seems to have made a misstep and fell across the track. The car passed over him severing his body intirely [sic] and carrying one half several feet beyond the other. Vassar was about 12 years of age—a nice manly [sic] little fellow. It appears when he started to climb on the car a gentleman called him not to do so but he did not heed the warning. The train was moving slowly at the time of the accident. The entire town deeply sympathizes with Mr. and Mrs. Brown in the sad affliction.

Editor Montgomery added this note: "Mr. Brown and his estimable lady have many friends in Sevierville and Sevier County who will remember their little boy as he used to play in his childish glee along the streets of Sevierville and all of us deeply sympathize with them in this sad misfortune."

Returning to the story of the cross, Herman Knowles said there have been three crosses to replace the original one put there by his father. The fourth and present one is made of steel and has been repainted by Newport Rescue Squad.

It may be true that the Indians used the promontory on which the cross stands as a lookout point. It may also be true, although it is not proven, that desperate lovers leapt to their deaths in the river below.

However, the true story of the erection of the cross in memory of Vassar Brown is a page from Newport's past.

The History of Grand View Sanatorium

In the early days of the twentieth century, tuberculosis was a dreaded disease. As medical treatment improved, effective tests and vaccines for a time have seemed to control it. Medical authorities, however, are now telling us that tuberculosis is reappearing, and is resistant to current medicines. Many of you may not know that there was once a tuberculosis treatment facility right here in Newport—Grand View Sanatorium—operated by Dr. James M. Masters.

The facility was located on the west side of Lincoln Avenue, between Second and Third Streets. Originally it was built as a hotel, during the days when the Newport Development Company planned to shift the town center to Eastport. The company's announcement for its big property sale in 1891 designated this particular spot for a "50-room hotel." In a Newport News item in the *Knoxville Tribune* on April 29, 1892, reference was made to C.E. Briggs, "genial proprietor of the magnificent new hotel being completed here."

The hotel apparently was not completed until late in 1895. Mrs. W.O. Mims wrote in 1953, "I was present at the grand opening of the Grand View Hotel and was feeling grand as a new bride." Mims had been married December 19, 1895.

The building was three stories. Offices and the main dining room (forty by sixty feet) were on the first floor, with the thirty-five guest rooms above. The building never really succeeded as a hotel because it was so far from the railroad and the main business district.

Dr. Masters desired to establish a place for the treatment of tuberculars. When he learned that this Newport property, worth about $50,000 then,

Grand View Sanatoria, later the Cherokee Hotel. *Courtesy of the Elna T. Milne Collection.*

Dr. J.M. Masters.
Courtesy of James P. Masters.

was for sale at $4,500, he decided to purchase it. Herbert Masters (1888–1989) recalled that the family moved here on October 11, 1899. Mims wrote that while Dr. Masters was converting the building into a sanatorium, the family lived in the Arthur house, which was later the home of the Anderson family.

Dr. James Madison Masters (1852–1924) was a native of Indiana. He was a graduate of the Miami Medical College in Cincinnati, Ohio. He and his wife, the former Kate Conner, moved from Indiana to Knoxville in the mid-1880s with their two oldest sons. Their remaining four sons were born in Knoxville. It was there, about 1889, that Dr. Masters began to specialize in the treatment of tuberculosis.

I have seen an advertising brochure about this facility:

Grand View Sanatoria
Devoted to the Treatment of Throat and Lung Affection
Management Dr. J.M. Masters, Medical Director.

This 3.5- by 6-inch pamphlet not only stressed the need for medical treatment of tuberculosis ("Under proper treatment and management, beginning in the early stages of the disease, ninety percent of cases of consumption can be cured"), but also detailed the operation of this facility.

Dr. Masters wrote, "Methods and not medicines must be discovered for eradication of the malady. The whole life of the patient must be changed, conditions permitting the development of the disease must be removed, and the individual placed under absolute control…it is imperative that all care, responsibilities, and burdens be removed from them. No where can these requirements be so fully carried out as in a Sanatorium."

What does absolute control mean? It means "absolute care in the smallest detail of their conduct: attention to diet, exercise, sleep, bathing, amount of clothing, conversation, amusement and many things in which the patient would be discreet."

No doubt, some of today's readers have heard that tuberculosis patients were treated by living outdoors year round. The brochure addresses that practice:

There is at present a wide spread belief that living out of doors in the open air, both day and night, is all that is necessary to overcome the disease. Thousands of patients are wasting their time following this delusion…Sick or well, every breath of air must be pure, but to expose debilitated consumptives to the hardships of tent or shack life in all kinds of weather is preposterous.

You may have noticed the word "sanatoria," which is plural for "sanatorium." Dr. Masters operated two facilities for treating his patients. The one in Newport was called the Parent Facility, and the other was called the Florida Institution, located at Port Orange near Daytona Beach. A glowing account of Dr. Masters and the Grand View Sanatoria appeared in the *Newport Plain Talk* on May 13, 1914, when the facilities were described as "among the best in the United States." The article further states, "Some years ago [1907] realizing the benefits of a mild and regular climate, he [Dr. Masters] established a second institution in Florida. The change has proved even more helpful than was thought possible."

How was Newport described?

Newport, Tenn., offers an almost perfect climate for six months of the year, from May 15th to November 1st. The location, near the junction of the French Broad and Pigeon Rivers, is unsurpassed; the breezes, from the mountains are delightfully cool and refreshing, no dust or smoke to contaminate the lungs. The scenery is extensive and fascinating— mountains, valleys, and winding streams present an ever changing picture of harmony and beauty.

On the first of November, a Pullman car was chartered to move the patients and staff from Newport to Port Orange. The route went from here to Asheville, on to Jacksonville and then down to Port Orange. The trip took one day. On May 15, the route was reversed. Mr. Herbert Masters said that when he was older, he went ahead several days before the help to open the facility.

What did all of this cost? From $23 to $30 per week, which included board, medicine and medical attention. Visiting friends and family paid $1 to $1.50 per day.

It is somewhat ironic that Dr. Masters received such a glowing tribute in May 1914 when he returned, for in the October 13, 1914 *Newport Plain Talk*, it was announced that Dr. Masters would be closing the Newport facility because he felt the Florida climate alone would best serve his patients.

Fire destroyed the building in 1926. *Courtesy of the Newport–Cocke County Museum.*

After the sanatorium closed, the building had various uses, but the dates of the ventures are approximate. At some time, probably right after it ceased being a sanatorium, two of the Masters brothers tried operating it as the Cherokee Hotel.

When Dr. E.E. Northcutt moved to Newport in 1917, he had his first infirmary in the building, but by 1921, he was located over the Merchants and Planters Bank.

At some point, the building was sold to the county board of education and was operated as a dormitory for students. This was true for the 1919–20 school year, according to the *Newport Plain Talk* of August 27, 1919: "The services of Mrs. Lizzie Dennis Hicks have been secured to operate the Cherokee Home. Mrs. Hicks will have full charge of the business management of the home—everything except the matter to discipline which will be handled by the teachers."

In reference to the above, readers must remember that that was before the days of school buses, and transportation to and from town was not as convenient as it is today. Boarding was the only option for those who wished to attend school in town.

The dormitory operation was not profitable either. About 1923, J.A. Susong purchased the building and attempted to operate it again as a hotel. I have a copy of an invitation to a dance there that was held on June 3, 1924, and I have seen in back issues of the local papers where persons hosted other social events there.

For at least the third time, an attempt to operate a hotel in the building was unsuccessful. When it burned down in March 30, 1926, it was being used as apartments and monthly roomers. Such a structure made a big fire. Some folks still remember it.

I have heard that much of the student body of Cocke County High School just left their classes and went to the fire, with the teachers calling for them to come back. Jim Franks said that Professor Hammer would not let any students from Newport Grammar School leave the campus unless they were going home for dinner. Franks said he just threw his dinner bag at his younger sister and headed toward home, which he never reached. He spent his dinner hour watching the fire.

The property on which the Grand View Sanatorium stood was sold as lots in 1939. The once imposing facility is now only a page from the past.

The Controversial Courthouse Debate

PART I

Of late, the courthouse of Cocke County has been the focus of some debate. In reviewing county history, it is evident that this is nothing new.

Cocke County was established by the Tennessee General Assembly on October 9, 1797, and this legislative act authorized the commissioners (or squires) of the first Court of Pleas and Quarter Sessions to establish a county seat and erect a courthouse. This was perhaps the beginning of Cocke County's political rivalries.

In the minutes of the Cocke County Quarterly Court, April 3, 1877, it was recorded that "the case of a county site [seat] has been a matter of contests, hard feelings and jargon ever since the county was established."

In writing about Senator William Cocke, for whom our county was named, Senator Kenneth McKellar said, "As already noted, Cocke County was named for him; and the good people of that county must have imbibed some of his pioneering and fighting spirit, as they have stormy political fights and feuds. They are a great people but they rarely agree."

It wasn't until October 23, 1799, that it was agreed to accept John Gilliland's offer of fifty acres along the French Broad River as a county seat. What early county history we have comes from W.J. McSween's *Recollections of Newport and Cocke County*, and McSween wrote that it took "many heated discussions" to reach a consensus. The first courthouse was a log building in the area now known as Oldtown.

This log courthouse apparently served the county for some twenty years. In the *Knoxville Register*, June 23, 1818, there appeared the following advertisement: "Bids wanted for a Brick Court House in New Port, Cocke

The brick building on the right is the Cocke County Courthouse at Oldtown. The log structure was once used as hotel, but possibly was the original log courthouse. *Courtesy of the Southern Historical Press.*

co: 42 feet long by 26 feet wide; 21 feet pitch; ground work of stone. Done by order of the commissioners. W.C. Roadman, Clerk."

Unfortunately, we do not now have any record of what it took the commissioners to reach the above order, but McSween dated that brick courthouse as about 1828, so perhaps it took ten years to get the project completed. John Weaver recorded that the bricks for this courthouse were made and laid by his ancestor, John (the Bricklayer) Allen from Cosby. This courthouse was standing until about 1908. When it was razed, the bricks were hauled to Eastport and used in a store building, which was operated by Solon Nease and later by Fred Campbell. That property was later acquired by Stokely's, which had it razed about 1971; some of the bricks from this are now at a home in Castle Heights. The stone on which the W.D. McSween plaque is mounted at the north end of the McSween Bridge is supposedly part of the stone foundation from this courthouse.

Fortunately, Mrs. O'Dell included a copy of a picture of the first brick courthouse in her book. Nearby is pictured the remains of a log structure, identified as the first hotel, but possibly it might have been the log courthouse. The site of these buildings is in Oldtown, immediately off Woodson Road and Highway 321.

Governor Hooper wrote an article about the controversy over the removal of the county seat that appeared in the *Newport Times*, November 23, 1938, and was reprinted later in the *Cocke County Banner*, March 2, 1972. In examining the facts that were included in the court case, it can be determined that the county jail was destroyed during the Civil War, and in July 1866 the county court determined that the courthouse was unsuitable. A committee was formed to determine the feasibility of extending the corporate limits of Newport the two miles over to the Big Pigeon River. It was further mentioned that the Cincinnati, Cumberland Gap and Charleston Railroad was completed to Clifton in 1867, and the commissioners appointed inspectors to hold an election as to whether Newport should incorporate Clifton.

The reason for such an election was to avoid a county-wide election, required by the state constitution, for removal of a county seat. By incorporating Clifton, the courthouse would just have been moved to another site in the same town, rather than the county seat itself having been moved.

The court case went on to say that on February 17, 1870, the dependents "fraudulently" obtained an act of the legislature extending the corporate limits of Newport to include Clifton, so as to indirectly remove the county seat. Newport, according to the brief, had no actual organization or corporate limits.

There is an order in the Chancery Court records that relates to this case, dated August 30, 1870: *Alex Stuart et al v. H.H. Baer et al.* The plaintiffs were the "Newport faction" and included Mr. Stuart Jas. C. Murray, Jas. C. LaRue, William Robinson, Abraham O'Dell, S.H. Inman and A.R. Garrison. The defendants, or "Clifton faction," included Baer, D.W. Stuart, C.F. Peterson, David H. Gorman, P.W. Anderson (County Court Clerk), M.S. Roadman (Clerk and Master), Wm Jack, G.W. Loyd, Robert Mantooth, A.A. Ragan (Register), D. Sprouse (Sheriff), J.R. Stanberry (Clerk of Circuit Court), Thos. Mooneyham, W. Phillips, Wiley Kelley (members of Quorum Court), Joel Ren (former Tax Collector) and Robert A. Ragan (Trustee).

In that case it was stated that (1) an effort is being made to remove the county site of Cocke County from Newport to Clifton (or Newport Depot); (2) public monies were illegally used to erect a jail in the latter named place; and (3) public records of the county are about to be removed to Clifton.

A response to this order was dated February 28, 1872, and the court officers were

> *strictly enjoined and inhibited under penalty of contempt of court, from removing or attempting to remove the papers, records of public property from Newport to Clifton or from holding or attempting to hold court for said county at Newport Depot, otherwise called Clifton…H.H. Baer,*

D.W. Stuart, C.F. Peterson and be injoined and inhibited from building or attempting to build a Courthouse or other public building for Cocke County…until further orders and decrees from this Honorable Court.

The Supreme Court decision mentioned by Governor Hooper was rendered in 1874, upholding the Chancery Court decision prohibiting the removal of the county seat until the required county-wide election was held.

Recent research raises a big question that more thorough research might answer: did the county fathers defy the court orders and remove the county seat to the Pigeon River?

On April 2, 1877, Mrs. Delilah Gorman, widow of Thomas S. Gorman, presented to the county court a copy of the account for the rents due him on the building at Newport Depot, which had been used as the courthouse of Cocke County. Major Gorman had presented the order to the October 1876 court and then died later that year. In Mrs. Gorman's request, it was stated that the said building was used as a courthouse from February 1, 1872, to December 30, 1876. (The court appropriated $320 to Mrs. Gorman.)

According to Mrs. O'Dell, the above courthouse was located at the corner of the present Mims Avenue and Main Street. (From 1908 to 1989, Merchants and Planters Bank occupied that site.) On the night of Friday, December 29, 1876, D.A. Mims, J.F. Stanberry, W.H. Penland and M.A. Driskill worked late into the night getting reports ready for the county court, which would meet on Monday, January 1, 1877. Before they left, they cleaned out the stove and laid a new fire. The ashes were dumped in a wooden box and it is apparently from this that the fire started. Only one book, apparently not in its rightful place, was not destroyed. It is now in the register of deed's office and is designated "Old 17."

An account of this fire appeared in the *Knoxville Weekly Whig*, January 10, 1877:

The Newport Fire
We learned from G.L. Ogden, Esq., of Newport, in Cocke County which is in the city, that the fire which occurred there on the night of the 29th of December…proved very disastrous and destructive to the citizens of Cocke county.

The fire broke out in the courthouse which was a two story frame building, and had gained too great headway before discovered to be checked and consequently, everything was consumed, court records and all papers connected with the business of the county. The Register's office being in the building, his records were also lost, together with a number of deeds belonging to various parties, which happened to be in the office.

The only thing saved was the books etc. of Squire Ogden's office, which were gotten out before the fire had reached his office.

This was truly a heavy loss to the citizens of Cocke County, one which they will not get over for years. A petition was gotten up and sent to Nashville and as was seen in our "special" Sunday morning, Mr. Duggan presented it together with a bill for their relief before the House of Representatives.

PART II

As scheduled, the Cocke County Quarterly Court met on Monday, January 1, 1877, just a couple of days after the courthouse fire had destroyed most of the county's records. The minutes of this court on Book 1 made note of the fire and immediately set about to reestablish and continue the county's business. The records of the county court exist from that date.

Unfortunately, the minutes do not record just where in "Newport Depot" the court members assembled on that day. Other than the business houses, the only other public buildings at that time would have been the Masonic Hall (still standing), the county jail or the Pisgah Presbyterian Church (which was then "out of town").

Records covering all this litigation would be found in the offices of the county court, the circuit court and the chancery court, but in order to construct a complete record of the dispute, it would be necessary to find them all and the restrictions of storage space over the years have rendered them difficult to find. This research will cover just the highlights.

Mrs. O'Dell wrote that the court first met in a shoe shop down near the mill, but this was to be only a temporary arrangement. The conflict over the actual location of the county seat was still being actively pursued. In the court minutes of April 3, 1877, in order to settle the dispute, the court ordered that "commissioners be appointed to lay off and establish with buts and boundaries and plat a county site [seat] somewhere between Newport Depot and the forks of the road leading to General Smith's farm or as near that place between Big Pigeon and French Broad."

The three commissioners were Dr. B.F. Bell, John M. Jones and George I. Thomas, but even though they were ordered to make a report at the next meeting, such does not appear in the court records.

The location preferred by the county court was probably in the vicinity of the present Newport City Park. Roads in 1877 were not all where they are today. The route from General Smith's to Newport Depot came across the bottoms and led over to a ferry, somewhere below the mill, that would carry passengers across the river.

Those who wanted to keep the county seat where it was were apparently working hard to achieve that goal. On October 2, 1877, the minutes report, "For the purpose of letting the Courts of Cocke County remain as they are at Newport Depot, the house now being built by J.J. Denton, near the Depot has been procured for the purpose of holding court therein until the litigation now pending shall be disposed."

Mrs. O'Dell said that this building was on the site now occupied by Tucker's Main Street Café. This building evidently could not house all the county offices, for the minutes of January 7, 1879, record that William Cureton was to be paid twenty dollars for twenty months' rent for the house used by the Register of Cocke County.

The year 1879 brought another attempt to move the county seat. On April 7, it was recorded that a preemptory writ of mandamus from a special meeting of the circuit court the previous February said that the county seat was to be legally moved to the J.C. Murray farm. This location is near Bridgeport and has been known for many years as the Walter Thomas farm. The court rejected this motion by a vote of fourteen to thirteen, and the next day ordered that a county-wide election be held to decide the location of the county seat.

The minutes of each meeting of the court began with listing its meeting location. In 1877, 1878 and 1879, the meetings were held at Newport Depot.

In January 1880, the court ordered that "the county site be moved from Newport Depot to Newport." Five commissioners were appointed to examine the old courthouse and report whether it was practical to repair. Those commissioners were D.B. McMahan, S.H. Inman, B.F. Bell, R.A. Justus and Morris Hartsell. At the April meeting, they reported: 1) the courthouse was too dilapidated to repair; 2) the only building there with adequate dimensions was the brick dwelling of W.C. Roadman; 3) it would cost $500 to remove partitions to make a room large enough to hold court; 4) rent would be $120 per year; 5) the court was not obligated to accept this report.

Apparently the court did not accept and decided to move, for the minutes of July and August 1880 show that they met in Newport, but the meetings of September, October and November were held at Newport Depot. In 1881, according to the minutes, the meetings seesawed from place to place.

A view from the high school hill about 1916 shows the courthouse. The store building across the street was Fagala Hall, temporarily used as the courthouse. *Courtesy of the Burnett Smith Collection.*

In January, July, October and December, the location was listed as Newport Depot and in February, March, April, June and November as Newport. In 1882, however, meetings through June were held in Newport Depot, and starting in July the meetings were back in "Old Newport."

There must have been talk about building a new courthouse. In April 1881, David Susong proposed to sell to the county bricks made in his kiln near Bridgeport for $200, as well as approximately 2,500 bushels of lime. The court rejected this offer, but later in July 1881 they accepted Susong's offer, but at a price of $5 per one thousand bricks, with no payment to be made until "the location of the county seat is finally determined." Also at that meeting, the court ordered another county-wide election to settle that question. (I could find no record that the similar election that had been ordered in 1879 was ever held.)

The minutes for January and March 1883 do not indicate exactly where the court met, but from April 1883 until October 1884, they met in old Newport.

On January 3, 1883, the court ordered J.S. Susong, administrator of the estate of David Susong, to produce the bricks. In the previous year, J.A. Clark had failed to count the bricks, so the court empowered

Commissioner W.R. Swagerty to do so. At the April meeting, Swagerty reported that there were 153,300 bricks. At the same meeting, the court ordered another county-wide election of the county seat, "In view of the insecurity of the present courthouse and the constant danger of the destruction of the public records now kept at the said courthouse."

Sheriff John A. Balch, in January 1884, was ordered by the court to hold a county-wide election for determining the location of the county seat on the first Thursday of August 1884. The records of the court in October 1884 show that the election was held on August 7, and 70 percent of the county's 2,898 qualified voters cast their votes. Of those, 1,637 wanted the county seat moved to Newport Depot and 384 desired that it remain at old Newport. After seventeen years, a final decision had been reached.

In the margin of the minutes, dated October 6, 1884, it is written: "The court is pleased to order and direct that county site of Cocke County retain its original name—that of Newport."

The next day the sheriff was ordered to move all papers from the courthouse at Newport to such a place in Newport Depot "that may be prepared for their reception." Also, the court voted to sell the old courthouse.

The place that was prepared, according to the court minutes, was the storehouse of J.H. Fagala, which served as the Cocke County Courthouse from October 1884 until July 1886. The Fagala building, on the northwest corner of East Main Street and Court Avenue, was razed in 1928 to build the Newport Laundry. The late Mr. Ivan Hogan helped to tear that old building down. He recalled in 1998 that it was built of twelve- by sixteen-foot pine planks.

PART III

Once the dispute over the location of the county seat was settled, the county court lost no time in making plans for a new courthouse. On November 3, 1884, J.Y. Jones, Alfred Knisley, James A. Clark, S.A. Burnett and W.J. McSween were given the task of securing plans and bids from interested persons.

Another consideration was the property on which to build the courthouse. On January 6, 1885, the court decreed that the new courthouse would be "built on the lot in Newport donated to the county by Thomas S. Gorman for that purpose, the lot being the one on which the county jail now stands." Major Gorman died in 1876, prior to the courthouse fire. This is the reason that the actual deed for the courthouse lot cannot now be found.

The jail was a brick building on the southeast corner of the present lot. This was possibly the structure that was erected with illegally appropriated monies, according to the 1874 lawsuit brought by the old Newport faction. This jail was used until the present courthouse was completed. The foundation stones from this jail were used to construct the wall in front of the Charles T. Rhyne Sr. home on Fourth Street.

Also on January 6, 1885, the courthouse plan submitted by Alfred Knisley was adopted by the court. It called for a building of two stories, constructed of brick, covered with iron, with a foundation of gravel and cement, two feet deep, with three feet of brick. The courtroom was to be eighteen by forty-five feet, with a twelve-foot vestibule, and four offices on each floor. E.S. Early, A. Knisley, J.A. Clark, D.A. Mims and S.A. Burnett were to advertise for bids in the Knoxville and Newport papers.

On April 6, 1885, the court records state the adopted courthouse plan to be the same plan that was used for the Blount County Courthouse in Maryville. Carpenter and Emrick's book *Tennessee Courthouses* reports that structure was designed by architect J.F. Bauman and built in 1880 at a cost of $12,779.01. The picture of this Blount County Courthouse so closely resembles the Cocke County building, even down to the ornamentation, that one might wonder if the picture had been mistakenly identified.

The next day, April 7, the detailed construction specifications for the courthouse were adopted by the court and recorded in the minutes. Even a diagram for the courtroom benches was included. A building committee composed of C.F. Boyer, D.A. Mims and S.A. Burnett had been appointed, but with the resignations of Mims and Burnett, J.C. Morell and J.H. Fagala were added.

On April 9, the construction contract was awarded to J.H. Randolph. It was included in the court minutes and signed by Randolph and William Moore, chairman of the county court. It specified that Randolph was to provide all necessary materials and "build with no delay of intermission except from necessities of weather a court house for the county of Cocke on the lot of late situated in Newport, Tennessee, between the residences of P.W. Anderson and C.F. Boyer." (That seems a strange way to designate the location. The Boyer home was on the corner of East Main and Court Avenue, where Manes' parking lot is now, and Anderson lived on the spot now occupied by attorneys Campbell, Hooper, Smith and Hurst.)

The building was to be completed by August 1, 1886, and $10,025 in bonds were to be issued for the project, which made it $2,700 cheaper than the Blount County Courthouse. The court minutes also noted that there was still a problem with the Susong bricks. In 1882, Randolph had agreed to take all the brick at the price the county had paid, and it may be surmised that the county had not paid the Susong estate, for mention of this matter included the phrase "a judgment outstanding against the county." Perhaps the county was waiting for Randolph to pay. Anyway, it was recorded that Randolph's debt would be included against the cost of construction.

The construction apparently went well, for on July 6, 1886, the building committee of Boyer, Morell and Fagala made their report to the court:

We the undersigned committee appointed by your worshipful body at the April term of this court 1885, for the purpose of superintending the building of a court house for the said county do hereby make the following report:

In our judgment, the walls, roofing and materials furnished and the matter of putting the same up and on are in our judgment in accordance with the plans and specifications with the exception of the following, to wit: the stairway in the rear of the building, the elevated seating in the courtroom, the walnut newel posts, the circular banisters around the bar, all of which changes being submitted and agreed to by your worshipful body. Judges stand, the mantles, plastering above the windows, also an insufficient number of seats. As to these last named, we respectfully submit them to you for your consideration.

The court then voted to accept the courthouse from Randolph, the contractor, "believing and knowing that the courthouse has been well built and honestly and beautifully finished." However, it was noted that Randolph still had to hang the window weights. Richard DeWitt was to be paid twenty-five cents per window to install locks and fasteners on the lower-story windows. Further business ordered him to erect two privies (six by ten feet) for the public, one for the men, the other for women, on the county jail lot. The court then voted to enclose the courthouse lot with an iron fence, specifying that the jail was to be on the outside of the said fence. The county officers were ordered to move their records, "the public welfare requiring it."

Without a doubt, the citizens of Newport and Cocke County were pleased with their new courthouse. With its three-story mansard tower, it was the most impressive building in the new county seat, representing a new beginning, now that its location had finally been settled.

Cocke County Courthouse,
1885–1930. *Courtesy of Dan Burnett.*

Time, as always, brought changes.

There was a problem with the privies and the city of Newport. On April 4, 1904, the minutes show that the city was ordered by the court to remove their calaboose "off the county lot at once and a public privy be erected on the spot where the calaboose now stands."

Apparently, the building was electrified in 1906. In the minutes of the county court, July 2, 1906, mention is made "in the matter of allowing the Missionary Baptist Church the use of the courthouse to hold meetings, Sunday schools, and prayer meetings and of putting in electric lights under an agreement made between the parties and C.F. Boyer Sheriff." It was at that time that First Baptist Church was constructing a new church. It seems that the church needed a temporary worship place, and in remuneration, probably the same electricians who wired the new church also wired the courthouse. (On April 1, 1912, it was recorded "in the matter of having the electric wiring fixed in the courthouse to conform with the fire insurance regulations, the court ordered the electric wiring of the courthouse abandoned and torn out entirely.")

Space became a problem because on January 7, 1908, R.P. Driskill, the superintendent of public instruction, was allowed exclusive use for an office of the building on the courthouse lot known as the "County Exhibit House." This little building was on the south side of the courthouse and was used as the school office for many years afterward.

Water for the courthouse and jail was supplied from a cistern. On January 1, 1912, a committee reported to the court that they had inspected the water cistern and found it to have been done according to contract.

Fireplace grates in each office originally heated the building, but these were later closed when the county installed stoves. Each year the court acted on the purchase of coal for the courthouse. One year, the sheriff was ordered to get the coal "before cold weather so that the trouble last winter will be avoided."

Part IV

The courthouse is the center of the county's business, as well as a central point within any county seat. Lots of activities take place on the courthouse grounds. Jim Franks recalls several experiences he had in the old courthouse. Once he attended court with this father, and he recalls the clicking of Attorney W.O. Mims's heels on the wood floor as he strode through the upstairs courtroom. Another time a "human fly" scaled the walls and, once on the roof, did a handstand. (The fellow did not tackle the tower.) In the summers a tent was erected on the southwest part of the lot, and there the Chautauqua programs were held. However, Mr. Franks also recalls that by that time, the building itself was becoming dilapidated.

Cocke County's courthouse eventually was no longer regarded as great and grand as it once had been. When it caught fire on May 19, 1930, most folks were not terribly upset. The report in the *Newport Plain Talk* the next day somewhat echoed those sentiments:

> *The courthouse is an old building having been erected in the eighties. It was not now a modern building and talk is already going the round that an entirely new and modern building should be erected instead of undertaking to repair the old building…*
>
> *The present building was erected in 1886, following a long legal fight over where the courthouse [should be located]…The building at that time was considered one of the handsomest courthouses in East Tennessee. As the years went by, more modern construction was taken up and the Cocke County building at the time of the fire was what might be considered old-fashioned and not capable of housing properly the business of the county.*

The fire was discovered about 2:30 in the morning when Chester Maloy and L. Mantooth saw flames coming from the tower. By the time the fire department arrived, the entire upper story was ablaze. The lower story suffered heavy water damage. The miraculous thing is that few of the county records were damaged, escaping a similar fate from the 1876 fire.

Local legend names a county official as having been responsible for setting the fire. While the official was not convicted, some of those who had gone on his surety bond had to shoulder that financial obligation. The official's connection with the fire has been spoken of quite freely over the years, even in his own presence. Forrest (Sockie) Templin was digging a ditch sometime later when the former official walked by and inquired as to what was being done. Sockie replied, "I'm trying to find the match you used to set the courthouse on fire!" (Those who remember Templin can attest to the likelihood of his saying that.)

The newspaper report credits a heavy downpour with making the fire less of a disaster. At that time, the *Plain Talk* was located near the courthouse and it was considered lucky that the building was spared, owing to the fact that it had a wooden roof. Embers had fallen as far away as Grandpa Allen's Store on West Main Street. The jail, of course, was not located in the courthouse, but Sheriff Mack Harper stated that he had been ready to liberate all of the prisoners, had the jail been in danger of burning.

The offices of trustee county court clerk, register of deeds, circuit court clerk and sheriff were moved to the B.D. Jones Building, which was located on the southeast corner of Broadway and Woodlawn (Johnson's Auto Repair is there now). The office of the superintendent of schools was not in the courthouse. It was in the adjacent Hooper and Cate building, and Superintendent Roy Campbell had moved the county agent into his office following the fire until larger quarters could be secured over Holder's Cash and Carry Store.

It was generally acknowledged that a new courthouse had to be built. Again there was a difference of opinion as to where it should be built. Those who wanted to move the site were told that the deed to the courthouse contained a clause designating it to be used only for a courthouse and jail. However, the deed could not be found, as it had been destroyed no doubt in 1876.

The *Plain Talk* interviewed several citizens whose responses appeared in the May 23 issue: Miss Edna Fisher, Dr. L.S. Nease, R.C. Minnis, A.G. Neas, Bruce Roberts, M.A. Roadman, George F. Smith, Rhea Seehorn, R.P. Clark, Maurice Ottinger, Tip Brown, B.H. Teague, John Ruble, Bud Willis, W.B. Harkins, Earl Smith, Hugh Holder, H.C. Mantooth and P.T. Bauman. With the exception of Earl Smith, all favored erecting a new courthouse and most suggested facing in on Back Street (Broadway), which was then the heavily traveled Dixie Highway. Tip Brown suggested a city-county building. Both George Smith and R.P. Clark did not feel

Present Cocke County Courthouse. *Courtesy of the Elna T. Milne Collection.*

Train #12 at the Newport Depot about 1915. *Courtesy of the Elna T. Milne Collection.*

that the county could afford such a building in light of the national financial situation.

An article by Attorney C.C. McNabb suggested that the county was actually in a good position to erect a courthouse. Some years before, $300,000 in bonds had been issued for highway construction, but the state had announced that $100,000 of that amount would be refunded to the county. McNabb stated that the county could issue courthouse construction bonds and let the refund from the state take care of the bonds' principal and interest. On May 26, the court voted to issue the bonds, which was done on December 1, 1930, for nineteen years.

The architect's drawing of the proposed new courthouse appeared in the July 4, 1930 issue of the *Plain Talk*. Manley and Young, Knoxville, were the architects and the contractor was H.C. Fonde. The courthouse would remain on the present site, and it was noted that both the Main Street and Church Street facades would be very similar, but that the courthouse would still face Main Street. The new structure was described to the public:

> *The structure will be of reinforced concrete frame and floors, with tile partitions, brick with terra cotta trim, offices on the first floor, offices and jury room on the second floor with the courtroom. The jail will be on the third floor, reached by an electric elevator from the sheriff's office and cut off by a steel door and gate on the first and second floor. The entire building will be fire proof, including metal trim for the doors and windows. The inside doors will be practically all the wood in the building.*

The old courthouse had to be razed before construction could begin on the new structure. Some of the bricks from the old building were used as filler in the walls of the new one. The building was ready for occupancy by March 5, 1931.

Again Cocke County is involved in a courthouse debate. Our courthouse is now seventy years olds, twenty-six years older than its predecessor. It was built before the age of electrical office equipment and the electrical system has been added to and added to. There are water problems from the roof and the sewers. There is unquestionably a need for more space, but how will all of these needs be dealt with? Will addition(s) to the present building solve the problem for the long term?

Because of its architecture, our courthouse is on the National Register of Historic Places. This is something of which to be proud. Let's hope that any additions will be first class ones, constructed to maintain the architectural integrity of the present building and not to leave it looking cobbled up. Hamblen County did a wonderful job with the addition to their courthouse. Sure county finances are tight these days, but no more so than in the depths of the Great Depression?

Will the controversial courthouse debate soon be a page from the past?

Author's note: After this article was written in 2001, an attractive wing was added to the west end of the present courthouse. The architectural integrity of the original structure was so well maintained that the casual observer might not immediately notice that the wing was a later addition.

After Several Unsuccessful Tries, the Railroad Finally Arrived in 1867

Probably every present citizen of Cocke County has had some connection with the railroad here, even if it was no more than having been stopped by a passing train. The railroad has been a vital part of this county for the past 138 years.

Railroad travel began in other parts of the country in the 1830s, but it wasn't until the 1850s that it came to East Tennessee. Lady Ruth O'Dell's book, *Over the Misty Blue Hills*, records that by 1857 a group of local citizens were stockholders in the Cincinnati, Charleston, and Cumberland Gap Railroad. O'Dell states that these stockholders lost their investments when the railroad went into the hands of a receivership.

The Civil War halted any hopes of railroad service to Cocke County, but soon after the war ended in 1865, efforts to bring trains to Newport resumed. In 1922, W.W. Langhorne, a former Newport attorney who was then living in Washington state, recalled that when he arrived in Cocke County in 1867, the railroad had only been completed as far as Leadvale.

In 1867, downtown Newport was only a tiny village with the homes of David Hays Gorman and Thomas Sandusky Gorman, and a mill. Later, as the settlement began to grow, it took the name Gorman's Depot, then Clifton and finally Newport when it officially became our county seat in 1884.

One legend claims that the first train of the Cincinnati, Charleston, and Cumberland Gap Railroad arrived in what is now Newport on December 24, 1867; another story claims that the train arrived during "roasting ear time." Regardless of the exact date, by August 8, 1868, the line reached Big Creek (now Del Rio); by the next year, service had been extended as far as Wolf Creek.

The CC&CG Railroad was sold to East Tennessee, Virginia, and Georgia Railroad in 1871. The following was taken from the *Morristown Gazette* of October 18, 1871: "The Cincinnati, Charleston, and Cumberland Gap Railroad has been sold by the State Railroad commissioners to the East Tennessee, Virginia, and Georgia Railroad for the sum of $300,000 in state bonds. The road is forty miles in length from Morristown to Wolf Creek."

Construction on the line was stalled for several years. Passengers had to go by foot, wagon or stagecoach between Wolf Creek and Paint Rock, North Carolina. Citizens greatly anticipated the line's completion. Newport's paper, the *Eastern Sentinel*, reported on March 24, 1881:

> *Maj. B.C. McCauley, Chief engineer on the Knoxville and Ohio Road, passed up the road with a force of hands Tuesday to survey and locate the missing link in that portion of the C,CG and C RR lying between Wolf Creek and Paint Rock. Mr. Charles Waring, City engineer of Knoxville, accompanied the party as assistant. Maj. McCauley informed us that it was the intention of the East Tennessee, Virginia, and Georgia Road to let this line out to contractors as soon as the survey had been completed. He proposes surveying three routes, one on the regular line from Wolf Creek to Paint Rock, one from the present terminus of the Buncombe line and Wolf Creek, and the other in the direction of Grass Creek. The company will then choose from the three the most practical route.*

The first route was chosen, and the line was completed to Asheville by 1882, the next year. The line still follows the same right of way as it did in 1867. In the early 1920s, a plan was adopted to build a spur around Newport, following the French Broad River from approximately Rankin to Bridgeport. Right of ways were purchased, but the spur was never built, possibly because of the steepness of the grade in the Rock Hill area. Sug O'Dell said that only a few years ago his family was able to reclaim the land that the railroad had purchased from them.

A notation in the minutes of the Cocke County Quarterly Court of January 5, 1886, states that the Riverside Railroad Company within two years would be completing a railroad up the Pigeon River Valley and Cosby Creek, terminating near the residence of John Dennis at the county line adjoining either Sevier County or North Carolina.

At some point, the Southern Railroad system (now Norfolk Southern) absorbed the ET,V and G railroad. Newport's depot was built in 1922 after its predecessor was torched by a disgruntled employee.

Construction on T&NC Railroad, February 13, 1902. *Courtesy of the Stokely Memorial Library.*

The Norfolk Southern still operates a freight service through Cocke County, but regular passenger service ended on December 5, 1968. At one time, six passenger trains daily passed through Newport: early morning, mid-afternoon and evening. Coal-fired trains served Newport until June 18, 1947, when diesel service arrived.

Another railroad was the East Tennessee and North Carolina, which operated from the eastern end of Newport to Crestmont in the mountains of Western North Carolina. The survey began in 1899, according to a report in *Knoxville's Journal and Tribune* on October 8, 1899:

> *A corps of civil engineers is now at work surveying and locating a right-of-way for a new line of railway to be built from Newport to Waynesville, NC. According to present surveys, it will follow the course of the Pigeon River through Cocke County. The project is backed by eastern capitalists who own mountain lands in the vicinity of Waynesville and desire to utilize the vast amount of timber on it. It is stated on good authority that the work will commence on the road by the first of the year. If no serious hitch is made in obtaining right-of-way the length of the road*

will be about seventy-five miles and will be one half of Cocke county. The citizens of Newport are very enthusiastic over the prospects and will lend every assistance possible to consummate the proposed scheme.

The T&NC received its charter on March 6, 1900. A notice in the *Morristown Gazette* on March 14, 1900, says that the capital stock was $50,000. By 1902, the T&NC was in full operation. The first superintendent of the railroad was P.T. Bauman, father of the late Mrs. Dutch Mason. Later superintendents were Andrew J. McMahan, W.J. Parks and H.S. Mantooth.

The line extended from a point just south of the intersection of Highway 70 and Edwina Road (Highway 73), where the depot was located. It continued back of the present Con-Agra Distribution Center and followed the hillside up a point known as the Foreman Curve (named for Joshua Foreman), where it basically followed the river up to a point east of the Rock Barn. There it crossed the bottoms, passed in back of the Wood Brothers store at Edwina and continued along the present road all the way through Wilton Springs, Denton, Bluffton and Hartford.

Much of the railroad route from Hartford to Waterville was obliterated by I-40. The T&NC line was never completed to Waynesville. About 1911, another company, the Transcontinental, attempted to build a railroad in North Carolina on the opposite side of the Pigeon River, but this project failed. Litigation between them and the T&NC company followed.

The T&NC operated both freight and passenger service, with three round-trip trains each day. Regularly scheduled stops occurred at Edwina, Wilton Springs, Denton, Bluffton, Hartford, Naillon, Browns, Waterville, Mount Sterling and Crestmont. Unscheduled stops depended on the whims of the passengers. A one-way trip took about an hour and fifteen minutes (if there were no unscheduled stops!).

This line ceased operations in 1938, and much of the railroad bed was converted into the present highway. A more complete history of this railroad can be found in *Ghost Railroads of Tennessee* by Elmer Sulzer.

Recent research indicates that relations were not always amicable with the railroad. A reprint of a Newport News article in the *Morristown Gazette* on December 21, 1892, entitled "Railroads," gives the following account:

During the past few weeks we have heard rumors of some half dozen railroad enterprises and some of them are likely to be realization, if our people will only have a little "get up and git" about them. Here we are at the mercy of one railroad corporation who charges us just such rates as

Railroad bridge in East Newport about 1909. The distant traffic bridge was replaced in 1936 by the John W. Fisher Bridge. *Courtesy of the Mary Rowe Ruble Collection.*

they have a mind, give you just such train service as suits their convenience, and just such accommodations, as our depot is a sample, which would insult a mining camp, yet we all sit quietly and submit when there are these opportunities for bettering our conditions. Let our citizens be up and looking after getting an opposition line in here and see how quickly E.T., Va and Ga will be looking after making things a little more agreeable for its patrons in the way of rate, depot, etc. Hon W.J. McSween has a communication for one corporation, Major Boyd has another road in view, while R.M. Randolph, with a corps of engineers, is looking after another. Why not get up a town meeting, discuss this railroad business, see which would be the most practical, most convenient, and then go to work and see what can be accomplished in the way of better railroad facilities.

One of the proposals was the Unaka and Nolichucky Railroad. The *Morristown Gazette* reported on September 30, 1891, that the city of Newport had unanimously voted to take $80,000 in stock in that line. This line was to be from Morristown to Erwin as part of the CC&CG line, which was part of the larger Nashville, Morristown, and Columbia line. Such a line proposed to open up East Tennessee to the timber and mineral interests in Western North Carolina. One of the leaders of this venture was Colonel J.L. Cain, whose local descendants include Tommie Samples, Jane Littleton and Tommy Smith.

The Morristown paper of May 10, 1893, quotes Colonel Cain as saying that the Unaka and Nolichucky Railroad hoped to begin construction by mid-August, if all the capital stock had been raised. Another article in that same issue reports:

Cocke County has now taken the bull by the horns for a fact, and the first cloud burst came on Tuesday last, May 2nd, at a place known as the "Briar Thicket" in and around the church at said place, where notwithstanding the raindrops which came in ceaseless number, there also reigned one of the most enthusiastic railroad rallies that the glorious Fourth district ever knew. The original route for the Unaka and Nolichucky railroad was via Warrensburg and Ottinger, thence to Caney Branch, and on to Erwin, the terminus of the road. Upon investigation by vice-president Cain, accompanied by chief engineer Mozier, it was ascertained that a more practical route in many respects can be had by leaving the W survey at the foot of Bird's Hill, crossing the river into Cocke County and thence by way of Parrottsville to Caney Branch. As soon as this report was whispered in the ears of the natives of Cocke, the "rustling" began for the road, which resulted in the assemblage above mentioned.

In defiance of rain and storm, the citizens came from the hedges and highways until there were present at the church three or four hundred people, ready and waiting for anything that meant railroad, if nothing but a stake with red figures on it. The Parrottsville delegation came with about twenty-five of her representative citizens, among whom were Prof. Monroe [of the Parrottsville High School], *Dr. Susong, Messrs. Kelley, Ottinger, Eisenhower, Driskill, and many other substantial and good citizens. Sheriff John Bible represented the lower end of the county.*

The above article also noted that Dr. Susong presented Colonel Cain with a private subscription amounting to $13,900, saying that if more was needed there was a "reserve fund waiting." It was also announced that there would be a meeting on May 6, and five thousand people were expected to be in attendance. At that point the surveying crews were nearly to Parrottsville. The reporter noted, "It is evident that Cocke county is in it to stay."

With the research stopping at that point, it is not known what happened to the Unaka and Nolichucky Railroad venture, other than it was never built. Perhaps the reasons for the failure can be uncovered at some later time.

Newport's Union Cemetery Provides Last Home for Thousands of Citizens

D eath is one of the certainties of life, and from the beginning of time, when a death occurred there followed the tasks of caring for the remains according to customs varying from culture to culture. In this part of the world, most families have chosen to return the bodies of their loved ones to the earth in cemeteries or graveyards, which are regarded as sacred spots. The largest of such spots in Cocke County is Union Cemetery, which was established in 1899.

Newport dates from 1867 as a viable community, with the arrival of the railroad. Up to that time and until the establishment of Union Cemetery, citizens were buried in the cemetery adjacent to Pisgah Presbyterian Church, the cemetery at Oldtown, church cemeteries scattered throughout the county or private family cemeteries

By the end of the nineteenth century, it was evident to the civic leaders of Newport that a need existed for a larger cemetery. Among the records of Union Cemetery is an order of intent, dated October 18, 1895, which reads:

> *We, the undersigned citizens of Newport, Tennessee, agree and bind ourselves to pay the sum of fifty dollars each for the purpose of purchasing a suitable tract or parcel of land to be used exclusively for a cemetery, the title to be invested in a board of Trustees, one chosen from each of the Christian churches of the town, together with the mayor of the town who shall act as chairman or president of the board.*

It also specified that one fourth of the stock would be held by each of the four churches: Presbyterian, Methodist Episcopal, Methodist

Newport's Union Cemetery Provides Last Home
for Thousands of Citizens

Original gate at Union Cemetery. Note the summerhouse at the end of the drive.
Courtesy of the Burnett Smith Collection.

Episcopal South and Baptist. Signing this document were W.H. Penland, C.B. Mims, R.E. Styll, Y.J. McMahan, J.P. Hedrick, W.C. Anderson, R.C. Smith, S.A. Burnett, H.N. Cate, J.M. Stuart, J.R. Shults, G.W. Willis, John W. Fisher, Oscar O'Neil, W.B. Robinson, D.M. Hampton, Ed C. Burnett and George W. Gorrell. Today only Robinson, Hampton, McMahan and Mims have lineal descendants living in Cocke County.

The next record is dated over three years later. The cause of the delay of the cemetery establishment is unknown. On May 25, 1899, the Charter of Incorporation was signed by Y.J. McMahan, G.W. Willis, J.W. Browning, C.A. Robeson and H.N. Cate. This was certified by the secretary of state in Nashville on June 9, 1899, and was duly recorded with Burnett Rowe, Cocke County register of deeds, on June 12, 1899.

The charter called for five representatives from each of the four churches. These men met on June 16, 1899, at the office of Attorney H.N. Cate in the Hooper-Cate Building adjacent to the courthouse, "for the purpose of perfecting a permanent organization of Union Cemetery Co." Mr. Cate was chosen temporary chairman of the body, and Reverend J.W. Browning the temporary secretary. The capitol stock was $24 per share, totaling $1,000. Mr. Cate was elected president of the

Board of Trustees, Alexander Ragan the vice-president and G.W. Willis the secretary treasurer.

The annual meeting was set for every third Friday in June at 7:30 p.m. The list of representatives at this organizational meeting differed slightly from those who had signed the order of intent. From the Baptist church were Y.J. McMahan, H.N. Cate and J.S. Susong. Representing the Methodist Episcopal church were C.A. Robeson, F.W. Parrott, Alexander Ragan and W.W. Bibee. The Methodist Episcopal South representatives were V.F. Deaton, J.W. Browning, M.G. Walker, J.H. Walker and E.S. Early. The Presbyterian church chose W.B. Robinson, G.W. Willis, O.G. Jones, J.H. Fagala and W.H. Baer as their representatives. Absent from the meeting were S.A. Burnett and J.A. Susong, both Baptists. For some unknown reason, only four people represented the Methodist Episcopal church until 1913.

On June 26, 1899, the directors accepted the proposition from J.C. Morell for ten acres of property at $100 per acre. The bulk of the property belonged to Morell, but a portion of it was owned by Sam D. Wilson and Hudson B. Anderson. On June 29, 1899, the board authorized the execution of notes totaling $100 plus interest: one year—J.C. Morell $365, Wilson and Anderson $135; two years—J.C. Morell $500.

With the property secured, the cemetery could be designed and partitioned. Although not noted in the minutes, C.B. McNabb, a local surveyor, drew the original plat, which was printed on heavy linen by the Indianapolis Blue Print Company. The original cemetery stretched from a line adjacent to today's Bicentennial Apartments on the west to the flagpoles on the east.

W.W. Bibee is reputed to have been the first person interred in the new cemetery. If so, he had evidently been buried elsewhere and his remains moved to Union, for he died August 8, 1898, prior to the purchase of the property. Even though the list of property sales is headed by the name of W.W. Bibee, there is no date of purchase recorded. The first dates of purchase were in October 1899. On November 8, 1899, the largest number of property sales on any one day in the history of the cemetery was recorded. Those buying lots were R.L. Talley, J.M. Stuart, R.E. Styll, Owen Harrison, C.A. Robeson, Oscar O'Neil, W.B. Robinson, D.M. Burke, W.W. Bibee Jr., Mrs. Mary Susong, J.A. Susong, O.G. Jones, J.C. Morell, J.C. and C.B. McNabb, J.H. and M.G. Walker, H.N. Cate, Reverend Charles Brown, G.W. Willis, V.F. Deaton, S.A. Burnett, Ed C. Burnett, G.F. Smith, D.H. Reid and Dr. E.G.E. Anderson. On that day, sales totaled $536. A twelve-grave lot along the driveway sold for $20; most other lots, which were also composed of twelve graves, sold for $15. A few smaller lots sold

Newport's Union Cemetery Provides Last Home
for Thousands of Citizens

for $7. An extra fifty cents was added to cover the expense of the deed.

The following day, November 9, 1899, the board authorized R.M. Randolph, a popular local auctioneer, to hold a public sale of cemetery lots on November 15. Cemetery records, however, indicate that only one sale was made that day, to Charlie Shelton. The lot cost fifteen dollars. After Randolph was paid five dollars for his services, the cemetery netted a ten-dollar profit.

Many property owners moved the remains of their family members to the new cemetery from other cemeteries.

W.W. Bibee was the first burial in the cemetery. *Courtesy of Anna Pratt.*

When strolling through the cemetery today, if you see a marker with a death date prior to 1899, you are looking at one of these graves.

On November 21, 1899, the board appointed a committee to confer with Wilson and Anderson about buying the strip of land "lying in front of the north side of the cemetery." This sale was eventually accomplished for seventy-five dollars and is the site of the present cemetery office and maintenance facilities.

At the meeting of April 6, 1900, the board discussed the cost of building a "neat 3 room house and cistern" for a caretaker on the property purchased from Wilson and Anderson. In October 1901, the contract for building the house was awarded to W.B. Smith for $400. In January 1902, Reverend F.M. Williams was hired as caretaker and overseer of the cemetery. Although there was still a bit of finishing work, the house was accepted in April 1902. By September of that year, Reverend Williams was dissatisfied with the arrangements, and the board allowed him to live in the house rent free and keep all fees for digging graves.

In August 1902, Mr. Morell called for $656.37 that was owed him. A $500 loan from Rhea Minnis was arranged, which left the cemetery still owing Morell $56.37. There is no record of him ever receiving the balance of the cemetery's debt to him.

In the center of the cemetery, a circular portion of the property was encircled by a driveway. A summer house was constructed there in 1905 by J.M. Fancher, at a cost of $428.

Although the board realized the need for future expansion, it was unsuccessful in an attempt to purchase five additional acres on the east side of the cemetery from Mr. Morell in 1901. Also that year, the board realized that the cemetery was in need of some cleaning and fixing up. On November 1, the board authorized that the sage grass be burned and blue grass be sown in its place. Also, the erection of a new fence separating the cemetery from the Morell property was authorized.

In 1910, Reverend Williams resigned, and J.H. Robinson was hired as sexton. Robinson served until at least 1915.

The board in 1913 voted to prohibit any wall or fence of any kind to be built inside the cemetery without special permission. (The minutes do not say whether Mrs. F.M. Greer received such permission to erect the wooden shed and light over Mr. Greer's grave in 1939.)

An iron fence was erected in front of the cemetery in 1915. This fence remained there until the 1970s. Also in 1915, the board voted to buy a tent and several folding chairs to use for funerals. They also discussed the grading, planting trees and improving the grounds. It seems humorous to us today to know that during that year, the public was asked to keep all livestock and chickens out of the cemetery.

In 1915, the county road commission was asked to macadamize the road leading from Woodlawn Avenue out to the cemetery. A house was built to store the funeral tent and chairs, and a wagon cover was purchased for use in throwing dirt from the graves. The main drive through the cemetery around the summer house was also macadamized.

A water system with spigots was installed in 1920 at a cost of $400. These spigots have since been removed.

In June 1923, a Cemetery Improvement Committee was formed, consisting of J.S. Susong, Mrs. John M. Jones, Mrs. G.F. Smith and Mrs. L.S. Allen. These ladies were all members of the Mothers' Club (later known as the Twentieth Century Club), which continued to be interested in beautifying the cemetery. One of their projects was planting a hedge of spirea along the north side of the property.

Another attempt to buy the adjacent Morell property came in 1924. A proposition to buy approximately seven acres of land on the east

Newport's Union Cemetery Provides Last Home
for Thousands of Citizens

Grave of Dr. John F. Stanbery, 1922. Note the gate in the distance. *Courtesy of the Viola Clark Collection.*

side and rear of the cemetery for $500 was made, but not approved by the board. In 1927, the driveways on either end of the cemetery were opened onto the street. Today, these driveways are known as Drive 1 and Drive 3.

In 1928, the gates were locked at night to keep the "loafing public" out.

By 1931, Joe Lewis had been hired as caretaker. He served until at least 1935, when Alfred Sweeten was elected to this position. In 1932, the caretaker's annual salary was $520. The caretaker's house was in need of repair, so in 1931 the board decided to build a new house at a cost not to exceed $1,250. However, the project ended up costing $1,652.90.

In 1940, the board voted to allow Mrs. F.M. Greer to purchase the summer house for $1,800. It was her plan to reinter Mr. Greer on this spot. However, the next year, the board rescinded that vote, much to Mrs. Greer's displeasure. Instead, the board ordered the building razed, the drive straightened and several lots carved out of the area.

In 1942, the board was finally able to purchase the adjacent Morell property for $2,000. Charles Morell had attempted to start his own cemetery, and a few lots still exist in that section that were deeded from him to the buyers. Today, this part of the cemetery lies between the flagpoles and Morell Springs Road. World War II's intervention prevented any extensive work being done on mapping and grading this property.

By 1941, the cemetery was in possession of approximately thirty acres of land behind the caretaker's residence. This property transfer satisfied a debt owed the cemetery by W.D. McSween. This acreage encompassed the area lying roughly between Beech Street and Washington Avenue and Mineral Street and Ninth Street. It was subdivided and sold at public auction on January 21, 1954, and brought $33,795 into the cemetery coffers.

Originally the board of directors had consisted of twenty members, five from each of the town's four major churches. In 1941, the Methodist Episcopal Church and Methodist Episcopal South Church merged to form First United Methodist. This move gave the Methodists ten members on the board. On June 17, 1946, the cemetery charter was amended to have five members each from the three churches, but not to remove any of the existing Methodist board members. Thus, it was not necessary to elect a Methodist board member until after the death of C.M. Babb in 1961.

In October 1950, Sheriff R.W. Smith offered the cemetery twelve acres of land across Morell Spring Road at $1,000 per acre. Three years later, Sheriff Smith's offer remained basically the same, and the board felt that when they sold the McSween property, they would be in a position to buy the Smith land. The option was $12,000 if Smith had the use of the property for three more years, or $12,500 if the cemetery took immediate possession. The latter deal was closed on October 26, 1953, with the Smiths receiving a six-grave lot when the property was plotted. However, Sheriff Smith died before this was done, and in 1968 the board settled with his widow on this matter.

In 1960, the board considered making the Smith property into a Memorial Garden similar to the one that had recently been established at Reidtown, but decided against it. In 1963, Shan Bush moved 38,425 cubic feet of dirt from the Smith property to fill in the lower part of the Morell property. However, it was not until 1970 that the board employed a person from the University of Tennessee to lay out this new portion of the cemetery. The first burial in this part of the cemetery was that of Clayton Bowman in 1980.

In 1979, Terry Hux was hired as superintendent to succeed Henry Alexander, who had held the position for thirty-five years. With Mr. Hux, the cemetery's operation moved into more modern techniques. Whereas Mr. Alexander had insisted that all graves be dug by hand, Hux authorized the use of a backhoe. Riding mowers replaced push mowers, the cemetery maps were updated and the cemetery records

Newport's Union Cemetery Provides Last Home
for Thousands of Citizens

Grave of the infant son of Mr. and Mrs. Henry Alexander, 1921. *Courtesy of the H.C. Alexander Collection.*

were computerized. Ellen Williamson, who succeeded Hux in 1999, continues to manage the daily operation of this spot, which has grown to over thirty acres.

Eighty-five directors have served the cemetery board in its history. Twenty of these served thirty or more years. John Holder and Henry Alexander, both of whom served fifty-eight years, hold the record of longest service. The current board consists of Roy T. Campbell Jr., president; L.C. Gregg, treasurer; James C. McSween, Charles Kickliter, Tommy Denton, Edward Williams, Sandy Burchette, Kenneth Porter, Eddie Walker, James Masters, Tip Brown, Bob Self, Phil Owns, Bill Agee and Charles Manes.

Union Cemetery is chartered by the State of Tennessee as a perpetual care facility, which ensures that the grounds of the cemetery will be maintained forever. Approximately thirty thousand gravesites remain available, so the burial needs of Newport and Cocke County can be handled for many years to come.

Industrial Development in Cocke County

PART I

Industry in Cocke County was somewhat limited until after World War II. Prior to the Civil War, it was virtually nonexistent here. An attempt will be made to discuss the local industries in terms of their sequence of arrival, although it will be difficult to be exact.

The livelihood of most early Cocke County citizens was based upon farming. There were a few craftsmen like carpenters, blacksmiths, saddlers, cabinetmakers and even a tinner, as well as some professionals, like doctors and lawyers. There were some very small industries, such as gristmills or Aaron Bible's tannery, which probably only employed one or two persons, mostly family members.

The first outside industry here was probably the railroad. Plans for a railroad were underway before the Civil War, but the Cumberland Gap line did not reach what is now Newport until 1867. It was another year before it got to Big Creek (Del Rio), and by 1870 was to Wolf Creek. However, it was 1882 before the line was completed all the way through Asheville. As far as employment, local labor was no doubt used to construct the railroad bed and to lay the tracks, but as for actually running the trains there would not have been a great deal of available jobs.

There was an early milling operation here. On the riverbank, David H. Gorman established a mill that actually might predate Newport itself, as well as the railroad. Judge James H. Randolph purchased the Gorman mill and enlarged it to plane lumber as well as grind grain. In 1893, this operation was sold to a partnership. In 1913, the operation

Jim Jones at an overshot mill, probably in the Del Rio vicinity. *Courtesy of the W. Nathan Jones Collection.*

Newport Mill and mill dam about 1915. *Courtesy of the Burnett Smith Collection.*

was incorporated by A.E. Sparks, B.D. Jones, J.G. Allen, E.S. Early and A.R. Swann. About 1902, the mill began generating electricity for the city. In 1925, this system was purchased by the Tennessee Public Service Commission. The mill closed for a period, but then reopened in 1935 as a farmers cooperative. In 1954, it was purchased by J.D. Sluder. In the early 1980s, Mrs. Sluder sold out to an operation from Siler City, North Carolina, which ended milling here and sold the property to the controversial Mr. Benfield, who used it for storing hazardous waste. The city owns the property now, the mill having been razed in 2004.

Not as large as the Newport Mill was, the City Mill was located at the intersection of Broadway and Cosby Highway. Some of those involved with that operation were Barton Warren, Charlie Morell, Estel Stokely, Elmer Jones, Horace Gooch, Murray Stokely and Carl Wood. In the mill's last years, Burnett Produce from Morristown ran the operation.

Another early industry was the Scottish Carolina Timber and Land Company, which arrived in 1884. In researching previous articles on this operation, I tried to pinpoint the exact date of its arrival. Quite unexpectedly, I later ran across a letter that had been printed in the *Cocke County Banner* on July 2, 1976, which gives a brief synopsis of the early days of the SCT&L. The letter was from W.M. Crawford, then living in Marshall, North Carolina, to his uncle W.H. Fine in Texas, and was dated February 26, 1885:

> *There is a large Scotch Company located there. They have bought about ten acres below the railroad bridge and have put a boon [sic] in the river to ketch [sic] logs. They intend to bring them down the river. They have bought a large amount of timber lands in Tennessee and North Carolina. They have built a railroad Switch and station for there [sic] own use it is sposed [sic] they are going to put up machinery of every kind there. They are a limited company but I do not know what the size of their capital.*

While the management and supervisors came from elsewhere, much of the manpower for cutting the timber and working the booms and sawmills was local. The Scottish operation ended here sometime in 1886.

On the heels of that operation, the Newport Development Company attempted to stimulate the local economy with Northern capital. In 1890, much of what is now known as Eastport was subdivided into lots and sold with the fanfare of much industry that would be located here—an electric light plant, a sash/door factory, a tobacco house, a tannery, brick works, a

Unaka Tannery during the flood of 1902. *Courtesy of the Oth Maddron Collection.*

furniture factory, a handle factory, a knitting mill and a box factory. In the immediate aftermath, only the tannery and the knitting mill came here.

The tannery, first known as the England and Bryan Company, began operations in November 1893, continuing on the same site until 1976. It has been reported that it was the efforts of C.F. Boyer and F.A. Lincoln—who could probably be dubbed Newport's first industrial recruiters—that brought the tanning operation here. Negotiations had begun as early as 1890, for a notice in the *Newport News* on September 3, 1980, stated that a tannery would probably be locating here. This article appeared in the *Knoxville Journal* on December 2, 1892: "The Bryant and England [sic] tannery is being pushed. The foundation of the main building was begun yesterday. This structure is 238 feet long and 40 wide and two stories high. The main stack is 120 feet high. For the present a ferry will connect this enterprise with Newport."

Later this operation was known as the England and Walton Company and was under the management of the Fisher family. Another name was the Unaka Tannery. In the last years, the proper name was the A.C. Lawrence Leather Company, but to locals it was always just "the tannery." In peak times, as many as 150 people were employed there. Initiated around the same time as the tannery, but a totally separate business, was the Chilhowie Extract Company, which produced tannic acid from chestnut wood. This industry was established in 1903 and continued until 1943, employing 90 people.

W.C. Ruble at the Chilhowee Extract Company. *Courtesy of the Tennessee Division of Forestry.*

Realizing that there was still valuable timber in the mountains, George M. Speigle from Philadelphia established a lumber company here in 1899. He first had his operation in Eastport, where Mac Boyer later had his coal yard next to the railroad underpass. Bill McSween recalled a lumber operation there, which he thought used the same sawmill as the Scottish company, moving it from its original site behind the present Riverview Baptist Church. In a few years, Speigle moved his operation to the western end of Newport. The area around the present White's Food used to be called Speigle Hill. In 1906, the operation became McCabe Lumber Company, and in 1926 it became Rhyne Lumber Company, having been obtained by Charles T. Rhyne Sr.

Another early lumber concern in Eastport was Babcock Lumber Company. Because of the lumber industry, the Tennessee and North Carolina Railroad was chartered in 1900 and construction of the line began shortly thereafter. It was in full operation by 1903, extending over twenty miles into the mountains and offering both passenger and freight service. However, its main function was to bring down to Newport the lumber that had been processed at the mill at Crestmont. Over the years, the operation was owned by different companies: first Catahoochee Lumber Company, then Pigeon River Lumber Company—which was

Speigle Lumber Company, later Rhyne Lumber Company, in 1921. *Courtesy of Patsy R. Williams.*

Lumber mill at Crestmont about 1915. *Courtesy of the Frances D. Mize Collection.*

sold to Champion Lumber Company in 1911—and finally the Suncrest Lumber Company. Logging operations were finished in this area, which is now part of the national park. The T&NC ended service in 1938.

Holloway and Hart were involved in the early years of the T&NC. The community of Hartford was named for John Hart, who had Hart Lumber Company there. An even larger operation was that of Boice Hardwood Company, owned by J.W. Bell and Cyrene Boice, which began operation in 1917. They had purchased twenty-four thousand acres of timber in Haywood and Macon Counties. The logging was contracted out, but the logs were brought to Hartford to be processed at the mill, which employed 118 men. This operation ended in 1928. Boice and Bell later bought the T&NC line.

Jesse A. Fisher opened the Newport Handle Factory in 1914 in Eastport, on a site later incorporated into the Stokely plant. The handle factory employed about twelve men and produced hickory handles of all types. Steve Wardrep was the manager, and the factory was still in operation in the mid-1920s.

Oscar H. Medlin had a small lumber operation, which he sold to Bruce Helm in 1931. After Mr. Helm's death, the business was taken over by his son-in-law, Hoyle Ratcliff, who expanded it. Much of the operation burned in 1975. Lowery Ratcliff has a concrete business there now.

PART II

The Stokely brothers and their mother began their canning operation in Jefferson County in the present Swansylvania community in 1898. Their canned goods were first shipped to Knoxville on steamboat on the French Broad River. Moving to Newport because of the availability of rail service in 1905, the operation, located in Eastport between Broadway and the railroad, remains today on the same site, although at first it did not encompass as much property as today.

The factory employed as many as eight hundred people in peak seasons, when canning a wide variety of products—peas, corn, pumpkins, tomatoes, beets, kraut, apples, potatoes, greens and beans. In 1933, the family purchased the Van Camp operation in Indianapolis, but it was not until 1944 that the name was changed to Stokely-Van Camp. Quaker purchased the business in 1983 and now it is owned by ConAgra. Occasionally, you'll still hear an old-timer refer to the site as "Stokely Brothers," but a lot of folks still call it "Stokely's."

There was another canning operation in Parrottsville from 1911 to 1917. The Nelson Canning Company employed thirty to forty persons and annually produced about six thousand cases of tomatoes. Dan Ragan thought that the Nelsons brothers, Will and Charlie, were only running this operation for the Stokely brothers, who were their first cousins. The cannery was on the creek behind the present post office. Once the workers went on strike in protest over their wages; they were paid five cents for every bucket of tomatoes they peeled. Mrs. Floyd Williams said

Stokely Brothers factory and office about 1920. *Courtesy of Sally M. Burnett.*

that even though the cannery was abandoned when her family moved to Parrottsville, there were still boxes of unused labels. She and her little friends used to like to cut out the pictures of the big red tomatoes.

The county has had several textile industries. The Newport Cotton Mill was on the corner of East Main Street and Lincoln Avenue. I have found no mention of when it opened, but its two hundred looms had been in operation a few years when it was sold at a trustee's sale in 1898 to Walton and Lewis of Philadelphia. The building was later taken over by Stokely's.

There was a knitting mill located on Commerce Street, which was parallel to Broadway and East Main Street. Later, Commerce Street ceased to exist when it was incorporated into the Stokely complex. Even when I was working there in the summers in the early 1970s, the building, used for storage, was still referred to as the "knitting mill."

Ralph Burnett had a sock factory at Huckleberry, which was about three miles east of Del Rio. This business was in operation until his death in 1931.

Lamons Hosiery Mill #2 was located on Duncan Street in Northport, and the area around it was sometimes referred to as the Knitting Mill Hollow. The business was owned by a Mr. Lamons of Greeneville and was managed by C.M. Gibson; it had one hundred knitting machines and thirty-five to forty employees. The building, owned by Winfield Kyker, burned April 19, 1931, and was never reopened.

Loudon Hosiery Mill, opened about 1920, was owned by Colonel Charles H. Bacon of Loudon, and Frank S. Robinson was sent here to oversee the construction of the mill, according to Mr. Ham Carey. Possibly the Dixie Hosiery Company was a successor to the Loudon Mill. Dixie Hosiery was in the brick building adjacent to Shoemaker's Florist. (Doug Shoemaker had that building razed in 1996.) The owner of Dixie Hosiery was Maurice W. Raulston. The Raulstons came here about 1930. Mrs. Ilie West moved her family here from Lenoir City in 1936, when she took the position as bookkeeper. Dixie Hosiery filed for bankruptcy in 1937, and the Raulstons moved to Kernersville, North Carolina. The mill was reorganized by a group of local men and operated several years longer. There was an attempt by B.C. Castile in 1950 to reopen the mill in a smaller building at the rear of the original site. An article then stated that the mill had been closed "about five years."

Reverend A.A. Haggard had a knitting mill in West End adjacent to the old West End School building. This mill, which went into operation on May 1, 1937, was hoping to produce three hundred dozen children's anklets daily. In fact, the mill was later used as the school building until the present building was finished in 1951.

Fielden Manufacturing Company opened here January 10, 1936, upstairs over Newport Grocery Company, which was on the site now occupied by East Tennessee Tire Company on Broadway. C.S. Fielden was the owner, and the company produced men's wash pants and women and girls' wash dresses. Their original goal was to employ up to seventy-five, but I have no idea how long they were in business.

There are three distinct periods during the past century when Cocke Countians left here because of the lack of jobs. In the early years, many moved to the Carolinas to work in the textile mills. During the Depression, there was an influx north to New Jersey and Ohio, where work was more available. Defense work during World War II opened up job opportunities elsewhere. Some of these folks returned home in time; others chose to stay in their new locations.

Between 1945 and 1955, only three new industries developed here. In 1946, Mayor Charles Rhyne Sr. persuaded Wood Products of Morristown to relocate here. They produced wood turnings, such as table legs and bedposts. First occupying the Caton Building on Wall Street, they moved to the present site on Asheville Highway in 1947. Charlie Staats was the manager. Following labor problems, the plant closed for a year. In 1956, Ernie Eastridge came here from Wytheville, Virginia, to manage the operation. His nephew Beattie Sapp came with him. In 1963, Eastridge's son-in-law, Jim Stout, joined the operation. The operation was totally owned by the Rhyne family when it ceased operations.

Overholt and Fowler Manufacturing Company was established in 1945 in Overholt Hardware with a tack hammer, scissors and a treadle sewing machine. They specialized in custom furniture upholstery and had three employees—Mr. and Mrs. Lesley (Chick) Fowler and Ike Gilliland. In two years, there were 25 employees. The business moved to west Main Street in 1951, and in 1953 was incorporated as Newport Manufacturing Company with shareholders being Colonel Rhyne, Clyde Driskill, Ben Ray, L.R. Fowler, Colonel Bullard and Lacy Myers. The industry produced upholstered recliners, rockers and sleeper sofas and employed 125 people, operating until about 1982.

Ben McDonald and Charlie Joye, college friends from Clemson University, came here in 1947 and established Newport Textile Mill, which produced tee shirts in the space previously occupied by Field Manufacturing. Even though they were only in business until 1951, both men found wives here. Charlie married Elizabeth Blazer and they returned to his hometown of Columbia, South Carolina. Ben married Eunice Holt and made Newport his home. He died in 1997.

It would be only fair to mention that not everyone here was enthusiastic about industrial development. Realizing that it would bring change, there were those who wanted Newport to stay just like it was. Some of you may have heard the story of a local industry that actually encouraged American Enka to locate elsewhere, in hopes that it would not interfere with the labor pool. Enka located at Lowland in Hamblen County in 1948.

Part III

There were those who felt that Cocke County had great potential and that industry was not developing like it could. We could offer a large labor pool, inexpensive power, low taxes and easy geographical access to the Eastern United States.

The local chamber of commerce had been previously organized before it was reorganized in 1951 with M.M. Bullard as president. One of its goals was to promote the development of industry here, and the chamber formed an Industrial Development Committee.

Allen T. Glenn, Congressman
B. Carroll Reece, James S.
Franks and Paul G. Freeman,
1954. *Courtesy of Imogene N.
Freeman.*

In 1954, A.T. Glenn, Jim Franks and Paul Freeman went to Washington in an attempt to stimulate industry in Cocke County. Jeter Ray, a Cocke County native who was a solicitor with the Department of Labor, arranged for the trio to have interviews with their congressional delegation—Senators Estes Kefauver and Albert Gore, and Representative B. Carroll Reece.

The men were hoping that Cocke County could qualify for government funding under the Maybank Act, which would provide monies for establishing industry. Franks recalled that both Kefauver and Reece were encouraging, but Gore was hesitant, fearing that this would only draw industry away from places where it was already established. (Such attitudes eventually led to Gore's defeat in 1970, as a majority of Tennessee voters were feeling he had lost touch with the "home folks.")

Senator Kefauver, a close friend of Bullard's, saw the need for an industrial recruiter and he referred to Bill Batt Jr. as a possibility. Batt's father had been head of the War Production Board during World War II. When contacted, young Batt was already employed in a similar position.

The newly formed Cocke County Industrial Commission then learned of George A. Bentley, a Pennsylvanian who was working in Middlesboro,

Kentucky. Franks, Burnett Shepherd and Luther Cooper went there to meet with Bentley, whom they learned was ready to leave Middlesboro because he refused to work where there were unions.

Bentley went to work for the local industrial commission on January 1, 1955. His job was to make industrial contacts and persuade them to visit Newport. Many folks will remember Mr. Bentley, who was a heavy-set fellow and walked with a cane, badly stooped from an automobile accident. Even though he was careless with his appearance, he was an accomplished recruiter. He had contacts all over the country and knew how to reach just the right people, usually starting with the head man.

Once the industries sent their representatives here, it was up to the industrial commission to convince them to locate here. Franks recalled a die plant from New Milford, Connecticut, which had been extensively damaged by a hurricane. Contacted by Mr. Bentley, the owner sent his two sons here to investigate Newport's offer. The men were entertained with a breakfast at the Rhea-Mims Hotel and were quite impressed with the opportunities here. However, in the end the father just would not agree to move south.

The first year that Bentley was here he made over sixty contracts, most of which were successful, but within ninety days in 1956, three industries announced a move to Newport: Wall-Tube, Chemtron and Heywood-Wakefield. Along with Bentley, Bullard too worked hard to get industry here and to help them to stay. The next fifteen years was a period of change and development for the town and county. New industries brought greater employment opportunities and an improved standard of living. This period could be compared to a time seventy years before when the Scottish company came, bringing workers from all different parts of the world. Mrs. W.O. Mims witnessed that time and wrote what an impression these people made on the life of little Newport. The 1950s were a similar time, with the influx of new people, many from the North. It was probably more difficult for them to adapt to Newport than the other way around. Some did not like it here and left as soon as possible. Others, however, fit right in and chose to stay, even when opportunities developed elsewhere. A lot of folks, both native and new, have helped to make Newport a better place in which to live and work.

Wall-Tube was the first plant to locate here from Plymouth, Michigan. One of the tobacco warehouses on the Knoxville Highway was converted for industrial use. The company produced small diameter stainless steel and nickel alloy tubing; metal furniture, such as Surfline, which is still found on many local patios and decks; and automotive parts for Chrysler, Ford and Chevrolet. This plant employed about four hundred people. Some of those who moved here with Wall-Tube were John Ault, Wiley McMinn, Bob Kisabeth, Tommy Cramb, Dick Hoff, Fred Lesley, Jim Lyke, Bob Gooding and Howard Hochstadt. This plant closed in 1983, and Falcon is now on that site.

Heywood-Wakefield from Gardner, Massachusetts, began production here in a new building on the former poor farm on May 1, 1957. Ralph Blackman was plant manager. This operation produced school furniture, transportation seating and some upholstered furniture. Others who came here were Andy Reid, Harry Reid, Ed Roberts, Joe Roberts, Kermit Boultinghouse and Frank Petrey. This plant, which employed around three hundred, ceased operations here in 1982.

When Chemtron located here in 1957, they were known as National Cylinder Gas Company. The name was changed in 1958. The production plant was located near Heywood-Wakefield, and there it manufactured chemicals used in the pharmaceutical industry, in cattle feed supplements and in plastic additives. Their research facility, administrative offices and library were housed at the Rock Hill Laboratory, which is currently in the local spotlight, though under another name. Some who transplanted here with Chemtron were Bud Prisk, Ervin Lehto, Chuck Long, John Kennedy and Joseph Dye. In all they employed about fifteen. Chemtron later became Arapahoe and then later Great Lakes.

In the latter part of 1956, Mr. Bentley left Newport because the city refused to provide adequate funding. During this interim period he was in Erwin, Tennessee, Corbin, Kentucky, and Elizabethton.

Mr. Bullard and his son, Ronnie, established Bullard Industries here in 1959 in the Clevenger Town Community. This plant produced upholstered chairs. It burned down in 1966.

Detroit-Gasket, which manufactured gaskets, came in 1960. Their first site of operation was on the Knoxville Highway adjacent to Wall-Tube. The next year they opened a second facility off the Morristown Highway, where in 1969 the two plants were consolidated. They employed about two hundred. Some who came here with this operation were Ed Kasper, Ralph Byars, Harry Ellison, Paul Fejer, Leo Misel, Carroll Doman and Tom Clark.

In 1963, Mr. Bentley returned and assisted in getting Vernco, Electro-Voice and Sonoco to come here. Vernco, headquartered in Columbia, Indiana, began production of home humidification equipment

M.M. Bullard. *Courtesy of the* Newport Plain Talk.

and air moving equipment in Newport in June 1964 in their facility on the present Verner Avenue. They employed about two hundred. Some affiliated with this industry were L.E. Sprouse and Don Foust.

Electro-Voice came here in 1964 and located next to Chemtron. They produced speaker systems, microphones, AM/FM stereos, amplifiers and receivers. Coming here from plants in Buchanan, Michigan, and Peoria, Illinois, were Gail Hemminger, Norm Pitchford, Andy Goehl, David Gottwald, Marc Johnson, Russell Planck and John Overly. E-V ended operation here in 2001.

Sonoco arrived in 1965 and was the first plant in the newly formed industrial park, established on the Rankin Road on the former Ward farm. They have had several expansions since then and continue on the same site. Sonoco manufactures paper products, particularly tubes and cores, and with their use of recycled papers, greatly assists with environmental protection. Howard Gandy was the first plant manager. Some others who have moved here with this concern are Russell King, Bill Boozer, Lawson Stanley, Tony King, Anthony Smith, Ashley Morris, Richard Gibson, Jim Martin, Bill Galloway, W.D. Gibson, Frankie Munn, Claude Mims, Troy Lee, Buddy Parker, Ronnie Holley, Tim Timmerman, Bill Connell, Eddie Lennon, Jim Money and Matt McCracken.

Mr. Bentley left again but returned in 1967 and this time helped to bring Newport Industrial Products from Akron, Ohio, here in 1968. They produced semi-pneumatic tires. This plant employed about 175 people. The plant manager was John Shogren. Also coming here with this industry were Fred Mobley and Bob Burton.

Bullard was responsible for bringing Newline, a subsidiary of Kroeler, which produced recliners. Opening here in 1969, the plant on Rankin

Road manufactured recliners and employed 250. The site was later the home of Spring Arbor.

Though they were not actually industries, there were two other developments that occurred during this time that were great improvements for the county. One was Jefferson-Cocke Utility District, which brought natural gas service to the area. This was created in 1959. The first manager was Don Martin and the first office was in the Memorial Building. Later Irvin Ludwig came here as manager and a new building was erected on the Morristown Highway in 1967.

The Cocke County Water Utility District, one of the first of its kind, went into operation in 1963. It was funded jointly by a federal grant and local revenue bonds. This provided municipal water to many parts of the county from the French Broad River. A treatment plant and storage facility were built off Jimtown Road in Eastport. The water tower can be seen from many areas. Gilbert Weddington and O'Dell Gray came here with this project.

This series of articles has covered the history of our industries up to about 1970. A lot of folks are still aware of the changes in the past thirty years, so perhaps these are not yet a page from the past.

PART IV

Back in the summer, "Page from the Past" featured some history on industrial development in Cocke County. Since then, some additional information has come to light that may be of interest to the readers. Soon after the earlier articles appeared, Judge Fred G. Morrison Jr. (probably remembered by most Newportians as "Freddy") of Raleigh, North Carolina, kindly sent some information concerning his family's involvement with Wood Products, which I had known nothing about.

The Morrison family had long been involved with wood. Gilbert M. Morrison, grandfather of Judge Morrison, had owned the Morristown Turnings Company from 1910 until his death in 1944. His was one of the few Morristown industries that survived the Great Depression. His connections helped bring wood industries to Morristown, one of which was Berkline. One of the highway bridges in Morristown was named in honor of G.M. Morrison.

Judge Morrison sent a copy of his certificate of incorporation for Wood Products, dated April 20, 1946, and signed by his father Fred G. Morrison and his father's brothers, Roy C. Morrison and James C. Morrison. The business was to manufacture—in whole or in part—furniture and other articles of wood. Their capital amounted to $25,000.

Wood Products eventually fell under the control of Rhyne Lumber Company, and Fred Morrison Sr. formed Newport Turning Company, which became M&C Woodworking Company when the family moved to Thomasville, North Carolina, in 1958. Mr. Morrison died in 1966 at only fifty-four years of age. Judge Morrison decided on a career in law rather than woodworking.

Another interesting bit of Newport history connected with the Morrisons is their restaurant, Ethel's Dining Room, which Mrs. Morrison operated out of their home on the corner of East Broadway and Filbert Street. They advertised "Home Cooking you'll enjoy, Home made pastries and desserts." Their noon meal cost $0.72, and the Sunday meals were $1.29, which included everything—drink, dessert, seconds and tax! Their T-bone steak dinner was $2.50, and country ham was only $2.00. The following guarantee also appeared: "If not the best place you've found yet, your money cheerfully refunded." From what I've heard from some who ate there, not a great deal of money had to be refunded.

Recently a collection of old issues of the *Newport Plain Talk* surfaced and in perusing them, I found some industrial history.

OCTOBER 3, 1903: "The Chair Factory is being enlarged by the addition of a two-story wing which will be used as the mashine [sic] room."

DECEMBER 14, 1905: Under "Bridgeport News": "John Brooks has his new sawmill in operation with Chas. Myclas as sawyer. They are doing a splendid business. Sheriff C.F. Boyer has his new mill in operation. Wm. Harvey is a straight honest man and will give the people good satisfaction."

Under "Costner News": "The mill agents are still working up in this country for families to go to Greenville [South Carolina]."

JANUARY 3, 1907:

> *H.C. & Creed Boyer to get cotton mill in operation in 60 days. When Mr. J.L. Erwin operated the mill, he bought the cotton yarn already manufactured and wove it into cloth. Mr. Boyer says it is a difficult matter to get the yarn which is scarce and very high and all the mills*

Workers at Wood Products. *Courtesy of Fred G. Morrison.*

that make it are making the greatest profits. Therefore, raw cotton will be shipped here, made into thread and then sent to the Asheville mill as fast as its made. About 50 hands will be needed. Investors in this operation are Joe Gorman, C.G. Holland, J.R. Seehorn, C.B. Mims, J.A. Fisher, Dick Cureton, W.B. Robinson, W.D. McSween, J.R. Stokely, A.E. Sparks, B.W.D. Gorrell, B.W. Hooper, S.R. McSween, and Y.J. McMahan.

JANUARY 10, 1907: Nough:

The people are all excited over the railroad. They are talking of running from Del Rio to the Gulf. It is rumored that it will be built and if so, it will help our country more than anything that has happened. Our mountain farms would be worth more, our timber and all the products of the farm. There are hundreds of dollars worth of cordwood on every farm in the mountains that would be valuable if we had a railroad so the farmers could get it out without so much expense.

It has been reported here today that the Pigeon River Lumber Co. will suspend operations on January 15th…Report has it the mill will be closed for an indefinite period…We have heard several reasons for the suspension but have been unable to get official information. One theory advanced is that they have shut down on account of a recent advance in freight rates on all railroads…The company had just begun sawing after a year's work of preparations. [This was the operation at Crestmont.]

JANUARY 17, 1907: "Prospects looks good for a big chair factory." [Headquarters for this company was Mebane, North Carolina.]

JUNE 27, 1907:

The Bellevue Cotton Mill is now in good running order and is making about a thousand pounds of thread daily. Six frames are in operation and others are being added as fast as hands can be secured. There are eighteen frames which in operation will manufacture 2500 pounds of thread daily. At present there are about thirty hands employed. Within the next few weeks there will be fifty and sixty given employment. Mr. Boyer, the manager, says home labor will be employed in preference to imported labor, and with the exception of four or five workmen, he hopes to employ local workers exclusively.

OCTOBER 17, 1907: "After nearly a month's shut-down the Newport Mill Co. resumed business yesterday and the electric lights are shining once more. We never know how fully to appreciate electric lights and other blessing until they are gone."

JANUARY 23, 1908: "The big million-dollar fiber mill at Canton, NC was started last Saturday. It is one of the biggest mills in the world. Several people from this place are employed there."

APRIL 2, 1908: "The fear that the Canton Mill would kill the fish seems to be unfounded. Great numbers of them are being caught about the bridge and dam, tho' they are small and principally suckers."

How Difficult Was It to Get to Morristown?

No one today considers going to Morristown difficult. The ease with which that trip can be made is probably taken for granted. Such was not always the case. A few local citizens can still remember when going to Morristown was a real journey.

For many years, the easiest way to get to Morristown was by train. The railroad reached Newport-on-the-Pigeon in 1867 and the trip took about two hours. As travel improved, the trip was made in about a half hour. Going by horseback would have been the next best choice, but the time required varied according to the weather and how long one had to wait for a ferry. Road conditions usually made travel by horse and buggy arduous.

Any chosen route to Morristown necessitated crossing a river. Going by way of Dutch Bottoms required crossing the French Broad. If you went through Bybee, you had to cross both the French Broad and the Nolichucky and, depending on where you lived, possibly the Pigeon. At places there were fords (shallow spots) to cross. A few brave souls who didn't mind getting wet rode their horses across the rivers, providing the water wasn't too high. Most folks opted for a ferry.

Harrison's Ferry operated into the 1920s. Mr. John Chilton, age eighty-nine of White Pine, recalls that the ferry ran from Taylor's Bend in Jefferson County across the French Broad to a point in Cocke County just downstream from Dutch Bottoms. (Harrison's Ferry Road bisects the town of Baneberry today.)

Taking that route to Morristown, after disembarking from the ferry, one traveled down the river on a dirt road (mud if it was wet!)

to Nina, and then went to White Pine on what is now Highway 113. From there, one went on to Morristown, albeit by a different route than today.

If you went through Bybee, there was a bridge across the Pigeon River at Newport in the early 1880s, but the following notice appeared in the *Eastern Sentinel* on July 5, 1883:

> *The Public is hereby notified that the bridge across Pigeon River at Newport Depot is unsafe and that the county assumes no responsibility for accidents of any kind which may happen.*
>
> *Isaac Allen*
> *Chairman County Court*

Another bridge was built, but this one washed away in the flood of 1902. It was replaced by the steel bridge, which was used until the McSween Bridge was opened in 1958. At Oldtown, the "modern steel" bridge was mostly washed away in 1916. It was rebuilt and used until 1975, when the Dr. Fred M. Valentine Bridge replaced it.

The Nolichucky River serves as the boundary between Cocke County and Hamblen County at Lowland. Mr. Lyman Ayers, age eighty-six, who lives nearby, says that there has always been a bridge across the river at that point during his lifetime. Apparently, however, there was a time when there was no bridge, for his mother once told him about the river being frozen so solid that even a wagon and team of oxen could cross over. The steel bridge was slightly upstream from the present concrete Dave Jones bridge, which was built about 1955.

Old Solomon's Ferry Road near Point Pleasant commemorates a ferry that crossed the Nolichucky to a point near River Road in Hamblen County. This was downstream from the present Hale Bridge and was still in operation in 1943, when Douglas Lake was built.

The maintenance of transportation routes has always been an issue with which towns and counties have had to contend. All able-bodied men of a certain age (possibly eighteen to fifty) had to either work on maintaining the roads a specified number of days each year or pay an equivalent tax. However, it wasn't until the advent of the automobile that really serious attention was given to the conditions of the roads.

A report in the *Morristown Gazette Mail*, September 4, 1929, stated that a new road was to be built between Newport and Morristown. One possible route was to run from Morristown to Oak Grove by way of Valley Home

Road, and then on to Newport through Reidtown. Another proposed route was to go from Morristown to Witt to White Pine.

As is known, the latter route was selected, but construction didn't start immediately. It was the time of the Great Depression, and money was not plentiful. The *Newport Plain Talk* reported that on February 20, 1931, a meeting was held in Middlesboro, Kentucky, to study what could be done to boost traffic flow through towns along Highway 25E (Pineville, Barbourville, Cumberland Gap, Tazewell, Bean Station, Morristown and Newport), which was one of the main routes to Florida but was being directed in other directions. Those attending came to Newport on March 3 when the Highway Committee of the Tennessee Legislature came through Newport on a highway inspection tour.

Another competing project was the Park-to-Park Highway, which was designed to link the Shenandoah National Park with Mammoth Cave Park and the Great Smoky Mountains National Park, but it was to come to Newport by way of Bristol and Greeneville. On April 4, 1931, Governor Hooper, Art Fisher, W.W. Jones and Frank W. Parrott attended a meeting in Washington, D.C., relating to this.

On May 6, 1932, it was reported that efforts were being made to relocate Highway 25E through Knoxville onto Gatlinburg, Bryson City and Augusta, Georgia. Soon after this announcement, the Newport Board of Mayor and Aldermen went on record opposing it.

In the midst of this, another major highway project was affecting Cocke County. Highway 25/70 was being constructed. This is the present highway from Dandridge. Today, spots of the original road, the 1932 road and I-40 can be seen simultaneously. This road was completed early in 1932, as seen from a report in the *Newport Plain Talk* on July 22, 1932:

> The *Newport-Dandridge highway is to be paved within the next year with federal funds…the pike road between Newport and Dandridge is being used at this time. However, the grade between these two towns has been completed for several months. Work was stopped because of a shortage of funds.*

The bridge over French Broad River at the Swann farm was not completed until the early fall of 1933. That bridge was named the Colonel A.R. Swann Bridge, and was in use until 2004. Occasionally you will hear a local person refer to that location as "Swann's" or "Swann's Bridge."

On August 26, 1932, it was reported:

> *The new Morristown highway seems to be assuming the proportions of reality…All land owners whose property will be cut by the highway have signed deeds to give the necessary land with the exception of one… The proposed highway will be a connecting link between Morristown and Newport and will cut off six miles on the trip. It will have scenic possibilities since it traverses the fertile Dutch Bottoms.*
>
> *The portion of the route which lies in Hamblen County is already graded. The portion which cuts Jefferson County will soon be under construction…Contract for a bridge, which will be thrown across the French Broad at the McNabb farm, will be let at an early date.*
>
> *As the county was devoid of road funds, the question was put directly to the property owners. The county is deeply indebted to these public spirited citizens who are making this new highway a possibility…*
>
> *According to W.C. Cureton, this project means that approximately a half million dollars will be expended on the bridge and that part of the road lying in this county. And also it will mean jobs for many persons in the county as plans are to use as much home labor as possible in the construction.*

The contract for the road was let on September 14, 1932. The money came from the Reconstruction Finance Corporation. Employees would be paid twenty cents an hour for unskilled labor and thirty cents for skilled. The work week would cover thirty hours.

Funds for the bridge did not come through for nearly a year. On August 25, 1933, it was reported that the state had released funds from the first federal money received. The notice states that the grading was almost completed and it was hoped that sufficient appropriation for paving would be forthcoming when the bridge was completed. According to the National Recovery Act, wages had increased. Unskilled labor now earned thirty cents per hour, while skilled workers collected forty cents an hour. It was expected that construction on the bridge would begin in a couple of months.

The new bridge, which cost $175,000, was opened for use on September 12, 1934, without any kind of ceremony. Although it has been renovated from time to time, for seventy-three years this bridge has served the people of this area. It was named for Reverend J.M. Walters, father of Senator "Hub" Walters, whose home was nearby.

The Kiwanis Club of Newport had planned to have a "bridge party" barbeque, but that plan never materialized. The *Plain Talk*

Looking upstream from Walters Bridge, 1942. *Courtesy of Jill Z. Stuart.*

Looking downstream from Walters Bridge, 1942. *Courtesy of Jill Z. Stuart.*

reporter lamented that the road leading to the bridge from Cocke County was not rocked, and that in bad weather it would be almost impassable. The Kiwanis Club took up this cause, and on September 28, 1934, it was reported that the Tennessee Highway Commission had relented and released funds for a thin coat of gravel to be put on the roadbed.

Reverend J.M. Walters.
Courtesy of the Stokely
Memorial Library.

Imagine a gravel road to Morristown! It was just that for three years. Mrs. Della McNabb, who has always lived in Dutch Bottoms, well remembers when the "new highway" was just a rock road. She also remembers the excitement when it was paved in 1937. On September 17, 1937, it was reported that Rea Construction Company, contractors for paving the Newport-Morristown Highway, had moved their office from White Pine to Newport. The office was in the old T&NC Railroad depot siding, and it was hoped that the work could be finished before cold weather set in.

All that work for such a short time! Less than five years later, the new road would be unnecessary when Douglas Lake came into existence. It was relocated a few yards north. Tennessee Valley Authority (TVA) was going to build the highway with the same specifications. The state wanted higher specifications and paid for the difference. Construction on the dam and the lake began on February 2, 1942. On February 19, 1943, the gates

Raising Walters Bridge, 1942.
Courtesy of Jill Z. Stuart.

Raising Walters Bridge, 1942. *Courtesy of Jill Z. Stuart.*

J.L. Caton looks over Dutch Bottoms after the creation of Douglas Lake. *Courtesy of the Elna T. Milne Collection.*

of the dam were closed and the lake began filling up. TVA had agreed that all work would be completed by July 1.

It was necessary to raise Walters Bridge 10 feet and to construct abutment wings on either end, which made the bridge 1,765 feet long. Mrs. Jill Stuart, a lifelong resident of White Pine, remembers this time. She went to see the work that was being done and has shared the pictures she took of Walters Bridge being raised in April 1942.

Perhaps now when we make the trip to Morristown, we will appreciate more its convenience. And when the lake is down, look for the remnants of that long-hoped-for highway, which can still be seen.

How Did Some Newport Streets Get Their Names?

S ome residents may not know the origin of the names of the various streets in Newport. Generally the names were designated by the actions of the city government or by whomever the developer of a particular area might have been. I may not be absolutely correct in my assumptions of the origins of the street names, but I feel that I am pretty close.

These names are not set in stone and can be changed if the right people are so minded. Broadway was once Church Street. Iris Place used to be Cherry Street. Mims Avenue was first Peck Avenue. It is good that the memory of some of our past citizens has been perpetuated through the street names.

While we are talking about street names, I'll air my personal disagreement with the names that were given to some of our streets and roads when the 911 system was installed. I feel that some of the names are inappropriate and undignified. For example, the street names in Parrottsville are all bird names, such as "Cockatiel," a bird that has probably never flown over Parrottsville.

I will defend the name of a road that was apparently unknown to many citizens before the massive renaming project: Pig Trot Road. That is the old, old name for this road, probably used for more than ninety years. It took its name from Pig Trot School, which was so named because the school was up on stilts at one end and the pigs "trotted" underneath it.

A search of the minutes of past city councils would probably reveal the origin of several street names.

BACK STREET
This is now known as BROADWAY, and since it is a federal highway, it is now more heavily traveled than Main Street. It also was once known as CHURCH STREET.

Main Street at Mims Avenue, 1954. *Courtesy of the Mary Rowe Ruble Collection.*

Broadway at McSween Avenue about 1910. Buildings shown are W.J. McSween Office, Methodist Episcopal church and Masonic Hall. *Courtesy of Edith A. Redmond.*

Broadway at White Oak Avenue, about 1950. *Courtesy of the Elna T. Milne Collection.*

Broadway at Cosby Highway, about 1950. *Courtesy of the Elna T. Milne Collection.*

Broadway at Baer Avenue, 1939. The city pumping station is on the right. Stokely Memorial Library is now on the site. *Courtesy of the Tennessee Division of Forestry.*

BAER AVENUE

Hardin H. Baer (1819–1898) was a Cocke County politician in the latter half of the last century. He served as circuit court clerk from 1872 to 1874. The Baer home was later occupied by Holder Funeral Home and is now part of the parking lot of Manes Funeral Home. Although the name is pronounced similarly to "bear," it is spelled incorrectly on the street sign.

BELTON AVENUE

Guy M. Belton was one of the officers in the Newport Development Company of 1891. In the earliest days of Newport, Belton Avenue was known as "the Morell Road" and was one of the main routes to Cosby.

COLLEGE STREET

No doubt, this street was named because both of Newport's schools were located on it, although neither is a college.

College Street about 1916. *Courtesy of the Burnett Smith Collection.*

DUNCAN STREET
I would guess that this street is named for George Duncan, one of the partners in Duncan and Greer Hardware. The Duncan home was at 281 North Street. Duncan Street is in the area that used to be called "Knitting Mill Hollow" because there was such an operation on the corner of Duncan and Smith Streets.

FAIR STREET
The old Appalachian fairgrounds were on the present site of Newport City Park.

FRONT STREET
This was an old name for Main Street, which "fronted" the railroad and along which were most of the businesses.

HURST STREET
This street goes through the J.C. Hurst farm, which was farmed by the sons Allen, Clevenger and Joe. Their sister was Lou Ellen Hurst Kerley, and LOU ELLEN STREET was named for her.

ISON LANE
Ron Ison was affiliated with the National Bank of Newport in the early 1970s. He and his wife Ginger built the first home on the street.

Main Street/Front Street looking east, about 1915. *Courtesy of the Elna T. Milne Collection.*

Main Street/Front Street looking west, about 1915. *Courtesy of the Elna T. Milne Collection.*

JEFFERSON AVENUE

Originally this street was called Mill Avenue because the Newport Mill is located on the north end. Miss Elizabeth Thomas spearheaded the move to get the name changed in the early 1970s because she felt that the original name was too common.

LACY W. VINSON DRIVE

Most people know the origin of this name. Vinson was the principal of the Newport Grammar School for thirty years. What some people may not remember was that the original name of this street, which was opened about 1962, was MAE HOLDER CIRCLE. Holder was the Cocke County voting registrar for many years.

LINCOLN AVENUE

Most people think this street was named for Abraham Lincoln. Wrong! It was named for Colonel F.A. Lincoln, who came here in the early 1890s and was instrumental in developing Eastport and securing the tannery for Newport. In 1935, the *Plain Talk* reported that Colonel Lincoln, age ninety, had been here for a visit.

McCABE STREET

Walter McCabe was the owner of the lumber company that later became Rhyne Lumber Company.

McMAHAN AVENUE

This street was probably named for Y.J. McMahan (1861–1939), once president of the Merchants and Planters Bank.

McNABB STREET

The Carl E. McNabb family lived at the corner of North and McNabb Streets. The family home was later converted into McBeth Apartments, which burned in 1970.

McSWEEN AVENUE

W.J. McSween (1848–1914) was a prominent Newport attorney and could possibly have been called our first county historian. His office was in the house later called Pioneer Apartments, on the site now occupied by the Myers law offices.

MIMS AVENUE

This street is often referred to as Grammar School Hill, but it was first officially called PECK AVENUE for Dr. Ed Peck, who once lived in the house that was occupied by the W.O. Mims family. After the death of C.B. Mims in 1938, the name was changed in honor of the Mims family. At the north end of the street were the Mims Store and Mims Hotel.

How Did Some Newport Streets Get Their Names?

Mims Avenue about 1912.
Courtesy of the Burnett Smith Collection.

MOORE STREET
The Lyle S. Moore family lived in the house at 121 Moore Street on the corner of Moore Street and North Street.

NORTHCUTT STREET
Dr. E.E. Northcutt was a physician here. He lived at 160 Clifton Heights in the house now occupied by the Habenicht family. The property extended to the present Northcutt Street. Dr. Northcutt's son Winston lived on this property.

RHEA STREET AND LUCIA STREET
These streets run through property that was once owned by Mrs. C.B. Mims, who was the former Lucia Rhea.

RICHLAND PARK
This was once the S.L. Rich farm. It was subdivided about 1957. The street names had family connections:
JUSTUS STREET: Hugh Rich married Dorothy Justus.
MORRIS STREET: Mrs. S.L Rich was the former Bertie Morris.
SEEHORN DRIVE: The Seehorn family owned the adjoining farm.
TEDDER DRIVE: Beatrice Rich married Cliff Tedder.

RUBLE STREET

I am just not sure which particular Ruble this was named for. John B. Ruble, a Newport merchant, was also president of Merchants and Planters Bank. His brother, W.C. Ruble, was superintendent of the Extract, and W.C. Ruble Jr. served as Newport's mayor.

SMITH STREET

The Alexander Smith family lived at the plantation Greenlawn at the western end of this street, near the site of the River View Apartments. On this same street was the home of Alexander Smith's grandson, W.R. Smith. Later this was the R.B. Hickey home.

WARFORD ROAD

This is one of the oldest roads in town. The War Ford was part of the Indian trails linking the upper and lower parts of the Cherokee kingdom.

WOODLAWN

This street was given its name in 1891 when the area was subdivided by Jones and Randolph. Later Mayor G.F. Smith named his home "Woodlawn" for the street.

Lower Woodlawn Avenue about 1915. The two-story building was the city hall. *Courtesy of the Burnett Smith Collection.*

History of Telephone Service in Newport

May 16, 2000, marked the fiftieth anniversary of dial telephone service in Newport, but the community has had telephones for well over a century. An item in the *Newport Plain Talk*, March 22, 1906, gives some history of this service:

> *Last Monday, H.E. (Jim) Holland bought the interest of Dr. Snoddy in the Newport Telephone Company and the entire system is now owned by the Holland family. The system was established about ten years ago by W.G. Snoddy and Charles Holland and they have improved it year after year until their lines stand in all directions and the property is a very desirable one.*
>
> *Mr. Holland has also established a system in Greeneville, which is almost as large as the Newport system and is owned entirely by him. The excellent service which has always characterized this system has made it one of the best in the state.*

In beginning research on this article, I had 1897 in the back of my mind as the date when the telephone service began in Newport. I have no idea where I learned that. The above article validated it, however.

Horace Estel Holland (1872–1954) was born at Del Rio. His parents were Charles Holland and Matilda Campbell. His brother was Dr. Charles G. Holland, one-time mayor of Newport. I am not sure whether he or his father started the telephone service with Dr. Snoddy, as they were both named Charles. H.E. Holland went by the nickname of "Jim," and

H.E. (Jim) Holland. *Courtesy of Charles H. Breeden.*

he was elected mayor of Greeneville in 1927. His grandson, Dr. Charles Holland Breeden of Oconomowoc, Wisconsin, sent some information about his grandfather, which appeared in the *American Telephone Journal,* May 16, 1925:

> *After living on a farm until he was twenty-five years old, Mr. Holland purchased a grocery business in Newport, Tenn., which he operated until 1897 when he organized the Newport Telephone Co. and built a telephone system in that community. He continued to operate this plant until the year 1919. In 1903 Mr. Holland built the Greeneville exchange which he has operated ever since.*

There were apparently competitive telephone systems here in the early years. The East Tennessee Telephone Company advertised its long-distance rates in the *Newport Times*, August 1898. The cost of a call from Newport to the following locations was: Chattanooga (forty cents), Cleveland (thirty-five cents), Dandridge (fifteen cents), Harriman (twenty-five cents), Loudon (twenty-five cents), Morristown (fifteen cents) and Del Rio (fifteen cents). There was no mention of whether these charges were per minute or per call.

The Newport Telephone Company became Peoples Telephone Company, which was owned by the Hollands, and the East Tennessee Telephone Company became the Cumberland Telephone Company. The Cumberland exchange was originally over Smith Drug Store, but in 1925 they moved up over the First National Bank. The Peoples exchange was located on Mims Avenue, upstairs in the building last occupied by Joe Bible.

Having a dual system was not always convenient. To be in touch with every telephone in town required subscribing to both systems and having separate telephones for each. Local advertisements for that period often indicated that businesses had "both phones." My grandparents had both systems. My grandmother said that she would sometimes get a call from someone on one system to relay a message to someone on the other system. I guess if you wished to call your next-door neighbor who was on the other system, it would have been a long-distance call. Mrs. Dean Lillard, a longtime telephone employee, says that Ashby Holland once told her that a call from system to system in Newport cost ten cents.

There were several rural telephone systems in the county in the early days. I have seen a contract, dated March 8, 1899, between Dr. J.H. Delozier of the Cosby Telephone Company and Dr. W.G. Snoddy of the Newport Telephone Company that agreed to provide telephone service from the England and Bryan Tannery to the Cosby Post Office. Such telephone service was limited. If the community happened to be on a main road where it was easy to string a line, there would probably be at least one telephone at the post office and one at the depot, if the community happened to be on the railroad.

Nathan Jones wrote in his book that his father and J.A. Moore installed the first telephone system in Del Rio about 1910. There were no operators, and every telephone was connected to the same line. Each phone had its own ring, but when one phone rang they all rang. I would imagine that customers were only able to converse with those on that line. These early systems worked on the same principle as a walkie-talkie.

O.F. (Dan) Ragan remembers that Parrottsville had a telephone system and that the telephones were powered by big batteries. He thought that the line extended from Parrottsville all the way to the Chuckey River, but that each family was responsible for running its own line. Mr. Ragan remembered hearing about one couple, Peter and Rachel Ottinger, who got sleepy and decided they wanted to go to bed and did not want to be bothered by the telephone. "Uncle Peter" just went outside on their porch and disconnected the line, which created quite a bit of concern in the community.

I found an article in the *Newport Plain Talk*, June 19, 1925, which mentioned the feasibility of consolidating the town telephone systems here. At that time, Murray Stokely was president of Peoples. The Cumberland system was taken into the Bell system in 1926, and in 1928 Bell bought the Peoples system, ending the dual telephone system here.

Mayor W.J. Parks made the last call on the People system at midnight on June 16, 1928, from the Creed's Café in Eastport to Police Chief Bill Bell. These same two men then made the first call on the new unified system.

The new exchange was located in the former office of the Cumberland exchange over the First National Bank. Imogene Agee was the business representative, Ruth Rightsell was the head operator and O.L. Cofeman was the service manager. The monthly telephone rates were: business (private), $4; business (party line), $3.50; residential (private), $2; residential (two-party line), $1.75; residential (four-party line), $1.50. In 1928, there were 266 customers; by 1929, there were 461.

We sometimes take for granted the ease with which our telephone service comes to us, but it has not always been so easy, particularly for those who worked for the telephone company. I have talked with two longtime employees who remember when telephone service was much different. Mrs. Geneva Ball began work as an operator in 1930, and Mrs. Dean Lillard began in 1945.

Both of these ladies worked when the exchange was over the present Newport Federal Bank. The switchboard was in the room to the left of the stairs. Mrs. Lillard said that there were only six hundred customers when she started. There were four sections of the switchboard, and each operator oversaw fifteen pairs of cords. When Mrs. Ball started there were only three sections. On the switchboard there was a slot for each number. There was a little flap over each slot. When that party rang the operator, the flap fell down. The operator plugged her "back cord" into that slot and said "number please" and then connected another cord to the number being called. The operator then rang that number. If all fifteen cords were in use, the customer could not reach the operator until one of the calls was terminated. The operator had a stick to push the numbed flaps back up into position. Saying "number please" became so automatic that Mrs. Ball said once she answered her home telephone that way.

Each operator had her own headset, which had a mouthpiece and an earplug and was connected to the switchboard. There was a ribbon that went around the neck. In the early days, these headsets weighed about five pounds and the mouthpiece was shaped like an inverted horn. As technology improved, the headsets got lighter, but Mrs. Lillard said that the ribbon would still cut into her neck and she would have to pad the spot where the earplug rested with tissue. For sanitation purposes, no one used another's headset.

Operators each had a number, and it was against company policy for them to reveal theirs names over the line. They could only give their number. It was a requirement that each operator memorize all of the telephone numbers so if the person who called asked for a name rather than a number to be rung, the operator be able to connect them. When the number of subscribers reached one thousand, the company no longer required that of the operators. That is when they added "Information." Callers would still ask to be connected to a name, and the operator would reply, "I'll connect you to Information." The different operators took turns working the Information position.

The operators had the capability to listen to any calls and could be privy to all sorts of local news and gossip. They were, of course, strictly forbidden to reveal anything they might have overheard. If they did, it was grounds for dismissal.

I read this story about a small-town operator in North Carolina. During World War II, a soldier had landed in California late in the evening. He placed a collect call to his mother. Of course, it was three hours later in North Carolina, which made it long past midnight. When the operator in that little town received the call, she refused to connect it, telling the California operator, "You tell 'Johnny' that his mother's gone to bed and to call her back in the morning." Mrs. Lillard said that something very similar could have happened here in Newport. She remembered that if someone called and asked to be connected to a certain person, the operator might respond, "She's not home right now. I just saw her go down the street." One time, my grandmother was trying to locate a child's

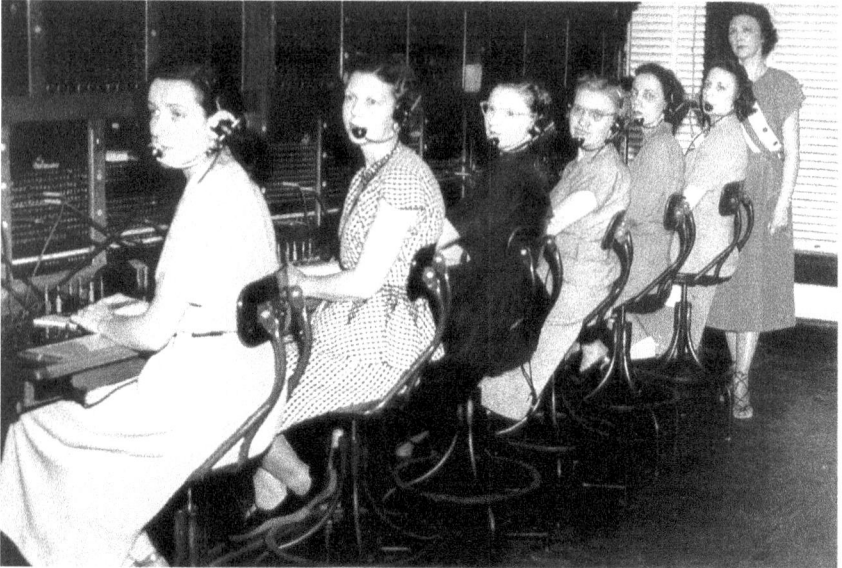

Telephone operators, about 1948. *From left*: Ruth Holt, Vaudie Lee Robinson, Dean Lillard, Imogene O'Dell, Dorothy Lillard and Irene Johnson. Standing is the supervisor, Beatrice Johnson. *Courtesy of Dean Lillard.*

costume pattern. She had called several ladies asking about it when finally the operator broke in and told her whom to call about it.

The operators worked regular shifts based upon seniority. Mrs. Lillard said that when she started, she worked "relief," the times when the others were off. Mrs. Irene Johnson usually worked the night shift from 10:00 p.m. to 7:00 a.m. Telephones were not as widely used at night as they are now, so there was a rollaway bed where the night operators could rest between calls. One night Vaudie Lee Robinson kept getting a drunk calling in wanting her to ring "Heaven." Finally she connected him to Art Fisher's "Promise Land!"

For long-distance calls, the operators had to "build circuits." That meant that they had to call another town and then the operator in that town would transfer the call to another point, and so on until the call reached its desired destination, where the local switchboard there would ring the number. A long-distance call was designated "MX Procedure." From Newport there was one direct circuit to Dandridge, two to Morristown, three to Knoxville and one to Asheville, Mrs. Lillard recalled. If all three Knoxville circuits were busy, then the next caller just had to wait.

Some of the ladies who have worked as operators are Imogene Agee O'Dell, Lena Mae Kennedy McNabb, Bama Kropff Johnson, Vaudie Lee Shults Robinson, Beatrice Smith Johnson, Geneva Kennedy Ball, Ruth Cooper Holt, Dean Murrell Lillard, Alice Ray Long, Aradia Buckner Overholt, Dorothy Lillard, Mamye Holland, Corrine Holland Davis, Lerneda Buckner, Marilyn Coon Ragan, Virginia Duncan Jaynes, Euretha Smallwood Carson, Carolyn Rowland Ramsey, Betty Lamb Self, Betty Lewis Freeman, Ginger Gray Smith, Diane Neas Whitson, Haroldene Thornton Layman, Janice Ball Ramsey, Tillie Cain Smith, Ola Gorman Hudson, Scottie Valentine Derry and Carolyn Styles Layman.

For many years, Kyle Johnson was in charge of the mechanical operation of the telephone system. Others who worked in this area were Charles Hightower, Donald Gorman, Dewey Ball, Homer Cabe and Charlie Dunn.

There was service to the rural areas in the early days, but those lines were usually privately owned and were eventually disbanded, leaving the rural citizens without Bell service. Mrs. Lillard recalled that when she started in 1945, there was an eight-party line to Swann's and the Swann family had both a Newport line and a Dandridge line. There was a rural line to Hartford that was owned solely by Mrs. Becky Callahan and maintained by Oscar Allen. The line was nailed on all sorts of things, like fence posts and trees. Parrottsville went on the Bell system on November 9, 1930, with six subscribers. Del Rio did not get on the Bell system until 1952.

In the latter 1940s, the Southern Bell established a separate business office here in Newport. Prior to that time the business office had been in Morristown, and Mrs. Beatrice Johnson, the chief operator, collected payments here at the exchange. The business office was down the hall from the exchange. Mrs. Bill (Marilyn) Ragan was first in charge of the business office. She left in 1952, and Mrs. Lillard replaced her.

The year 1950 was an important one for telephone service in Newport, as it marks when we were converted to the dial system. A new exchange was constructed on Lakeview Street and the business office moved into the former exchange in the Newport Federal building. Dial service was inaugurated with a "switch-over program and banquet" on May 16 at the Memorial Building, sponsored by the Public Affairs Committee of the Newport Kiwanis Club; Eddie Sklar was the committee chairman. The first dial call was made by Mayor W.C. Ruble Jr.

In 1956, Ralph Houston came here as the first group manager; prior to that, group managers had been based in Morristown. While Houston was

Operation center on Lakeview Street, 1950. *Courtesy of Dean Lillard.*

here, the business office moved to their new quarters next to the McSween Bridge in 1960. Houston left in 1964, and successive group managers were Niles Kitchen, T.W. (Bill) Granger, W.N. Calvert and Mrs. Billie Shirk. When Mrs. Shirk left, Newport no longer had a group manager, but Mrs. Carolyn Ramsey was named supervisor. The business office here was eventually closed and moved back to Morristown, leaving only a phone center here on Cosby Highway. The phone center was closed about 1982.

There were many people who would have liked to have had telephone service who were unable to get it. Mrs. Lillard had to keep a log of every request; telephone officials never quite believed there was that great a demand for telephone service.

One of the events that helped to get more service to the area was the visit of President Harry Truman to the Ramp Festival in 1955. Southern Bell strung a six-pair cable from Newport to Shangri-La Hill, where they installed six pay phones for the media's use. Mrs. Lillard was sent up with a cash box to make change for the reporters and to assist them in making their calls. Most, however, made collect calls.

After the festival was over, the Cosby citizens did not want the cable removed, so the phone booths were installed up and down the highway.

They were to be outside, well lit and available to the public. Mrs. Lillard recalls the ones that were at Padgett's Store, Wal Large's Store, R.V. Denton's Store and the Black Bear Restaurant.

After that time, Southern Bell sent a crew here to canvass the county and determine the desire for telephone service. They were amazed at how many citizens wanted it, so they began installing the four- and eight-party lines in the county. Many citizens will recall those and now wonder how they ever endured such inconvenience. Mrs. Lillard thinks that by about 1963, most party lines were two-party. Further improvements began in 1972, and by 1974 most rural customers were able to have private lines.

My research has found that telephone service received area codes in 1961, and in 1963 direct long-distance dialing was added.

The citizens of the Waterville community had a hard time getting telephone service. It was deemed too difficult to bring service over the mountains, and there was considerable red tape involved with the Newport system crossing the state line. There were a few places with phones in Waterville, but to reach them, the operator had to call Asheville, whose exchange had to call Canton, who then rang the Waterville phones. All of this came to an end in December 1973, when service was extended from Newport.

Today our telephone service is mainly computerized, and the voices we hear from our provider are usually recorded. The day of the personal touch of an operator saying, "number please" is a page from the past.

A History of Carson Springs

PART I

At one time—next to Newport, and possibly Parrottsville—Carson Springs was the best-known community in Cocke County. It was a popular vacation resort, and folks came from lots of places to escape the summer heat and drink of the mineral waters from the springs. Even today, its terrain is some of the loveliest in the county.

Some maps refer to the creek itself as Carson Creek. Correctly, it is Sinking Creek, which forms at the falls on English Mountain. The stream flows downward through the community of Carson Springs, sometimes visible from the present road, sometimes not.

It is south of the present Highway 25/70 until near Clayton Mobile Homes, where it goes under the highway and behind the tobacco warehouse and Falcon, where it crosses again to flow in front of the fairgrounds. It curves again and goes under the Sinking Creek Bridge and down into the river bottoms, where it flows into Pigeon just north of the wastewater treatment plant. The foundation for this research will be articles that Governor Ben W. Hooper wrote from time to time in the local newspapers.

The name "Carson" comes from Samuel Carson (1768–1850), who was granted ten acres on the waters of Sinking Creek by the State of Tennessee on October 19, 1816. In this grant, mention was also made that the tract had been surveyed on September 30, 1816, and that it contained a "yellow spring." (Cocke County Deed Book 2, 146)

In 1851, this tract was sold for back taxes (fifteen cents) and was purchased by James H. Carson for four dollars, the amount of the tax indebtedness and costs. The deed for this was issued December 7, 1853. James H. Carson was a son-in-law of Samuel Carson, having married Lavina Carson, Samuel's daughter.

The next transaction was on October 8, 1885, when the heirs of James H. Carson, deceased, conveyed the ten acres owned by Walter P. Carson. (Deed Book 7, 242–45) Because James H. Carson had no issue, the following heirs are probably siblings or children of his siblings: Samuel A. Carson, R.N. Carson and wife Eliza and Robert Owen and wife Emma (all from Jefferson County); Margaret Scruggs (from Georgia); R.P. Scruggs (from Iredell County, North Carolina); and John A. Scruggs (from Webster County, Missouri).

Long before Walter P. Carson began developing Carson Springs, others knew about it. An Indian trail is supposed to have passed right by the springs. In the *Morristown Gazette* on July 25, 1888, a correspondent identified only as E.A.S. wrote,

> *Forty years ago I spent a summer at Carson Springs, and thought it so beautiful that the foot of man seemed almost desecration. "The grove was God's own temple," was my first thought as I looked at the magnificent forest above the spring, with mountains on each side. The sublime solitude would have been terrible had not the notes of a thrush and the music of the gurgling stream…given life to the stillness. Forty years ago a few log cabins were the only footprints of man.*

Mrs. W.O. Mims, as a girl, lived in the present Wilsonville in the 1870s. In the *Newport Times*, September 18, 1940, she wrote, "The 'Main Street' of Wilsonville was the road meandering along up the banks of Sinking Creek and on beyond. Two hours of steady plodding over drifts of water and stones brought either man or beast to the Yellow Springs now called Carson Springs which even then was a popular resort."

With today's improved transportation, it seems incredible that it could take two hours to travel the four miles from Wilsonville to the head of Carsons.

Another early mention of the resort was made in a local newspaper, *Eastern Sentinel*, on August 12, 1880: "Mr. J.A. Woodside, one of the proprietors of the Yellow Springs made us a pleasant call Tuesday. Everybody returning from this favorite summering place seems delighted with the accommodations."

ROGERS' HOUSE,
CARSON-:-SPRINGS,
James M. Rodgers, Pro.

Five Miles from Newport, Tenn.

Good Substantial Fare. Purest Mountain Air.
Thermometer from 60 to 70 Degrees.
Daily Hack from Newport and no Mountain to
Cross.
RATES.—Per Month, $20; Per Week, $6. Children at Half Price.

OPEN JUNE 1st, 1887.
Address,
JAMES M. RODGERS,
Carson Springs, via. Newport, Tenn

Advertisement from the *Morristown Gazette*, May 11, 1887.

As far as development was concerned, Governor Hooper recalled that more of the land in Carson Springs "proper" actually had belonged to Major William McSween. I realize that this may not be precise, but the Carson tract was on both sides of the present road roughly from the lower spring (which is below the last bridge) up to the lower portion of the Carson Springs Loop. The McSween tract started below the lower spring and went up onto the sides of the mountain, surrounding the Carson tract. The property inside of the loop originally belonged to the McSweens.

One of the first transactions of the development was ten acres from Major McSween to Mrs. Sue E. Susong on October 1, 1885, for $77.50. The deed gave the right to "go and return from the upper yellow spring tract and use the waters of the same." On August 17 of the next year, Mrs. Susong bought three and a half acres from W.P. Carson for $78.75.

Over the next few years, there is a record of numerous sales of "lots" from W.P. Carson to various citizens, including J.R. Harrison, James H. Robinson, H.L.W. Taylor, C.E. Dunn, A.T.C. Bettis, Mrs. Jodie Jones, I.W.R. Franklin, Joseph Blackburn, Eugene Eckel, William Jack, R.W. Kyte, A.R. Swann,

J.R.N., W.B. Robinson, G.W. Hill, C.B. Mims, John B. Stokely, J.P. Robinson, Will Moser, Geo. C. William, W.A. Moore, J.L. Chilton, Mary K. McSween, Nannie Robinson Carson, R.A. Davis and W.R. Swagerty.

Of the original purchases, the one that stayed longest in the possession of the family was the I.W.R. Franklin tract, which was owned by his granddaughter, Eugenia Franklin Henry of Signal Mountain, until 1995.

Other notable purchases are those by James M. Rogers. On August 27, 1887, he purchased a lot from W.P. Carson and then on November 6, 1889, he purchased five acres from William McSween. Then, in 1889, Charles T. Peterson purchased property from W.P. Carson. Rogers and Peterson both had hotels there in the early days. Rogers's establishment may have opened before he actually got a deed to the property, for the advertisement reprinted here was from the *Morristown Gazette* on May 11, 1887.

In the previously mentioned account by "E.A.S.," some indication of the location of the Rogers House is given when it states that "a strong, clear mountain stream gurgles rapidly in front of the well-known Lithia Spring and the Rogers House." The Lithia Spring is what is now known as the Lower Spring, so I am inclined to think that the Rogers House was located just across from the spring, where the Hooper cottage was once located.

Another report from Carson Springs, dated July 4, 1888, in the *Morristown Gazette*, says this about the Rogers House and Carson Springs:

> *Arriving at Newport on the morning train from Morristown, which reaches Newport a little after 9 o'clock, one takes a comfortable hack and after driving over a good mountain road for six miles is finally rewarded by hearing the welcome, resonant dinner bell as the horses pull up at the Rogers House. After a hearty dinner new comers take in the place…*
>
> *The Rogers House is simply an old time country tavern with a world of geniality pervading it. The table is not excelled by any hotel in Morristown, and the Lithia water is conducive to a splendid appetite…A large number of guests are now at the Hotel, and before the season is over it will be filled to its capacity. Mr. Rogers and his estimable sister and associate in the management of the hotel do everything in their power to make their guests comfortable and content and the outlook for Carson's Springs is very pleasing to them.*

The Peterson Hotel was first operated by Charles and Mattie Peterson, Yankees who arrived here shortly after the Civil War. They first operated out of a building on the southwest corner of McSween Avenue and Main

Peterson Hotel, 1912. *Courtesy of Beverly C. Little.*

Street, where the Bob Hill building is now. They had a store there, and Mr. Peterson served a term as Newport's postmaster.

Mrs. Mims recalled that Mrs. Peterson seemed to be doing most of the work in the store, as Mr. Peterson supposedly had health problems. However, he outlived his wife, dying in 1907 at the age of eighty-four. Mrs. Mims also remembered the "the Petersons at Carson Springs…kept a very good table with plenty of seasonable food."

A portion of the Peterson Hotel is still standing at 1016 Carson Loop Road. The place was still being used as a hotel as late as 1939, when it was advertised under the management of Mrs. Wade Giles.

PART II

In addition to the cooler temperatures of the region, the water of the springs also created the resort that became known as Carson Springs. The area is approximately one thousand feet higher in elevation than Newport, and even now the temperature is usually ten degrees cooler there than in town.

In the *Prospectus* of the Newport Development Company in 1891, when an attempt was being made to propose the desirability of the town and its opportunities, this was written: "A few miles distant in the English Mountain is the famous Carson spring, at which place 300 people from the South spend the summer to take advantage of the curative qualities of these springs."

First, it needs to be emphasized here that there were two major springs in the area. These were generally called the Lower Spring and the Upper Spring. The Lower Spring is located on the left of the present road, just before crossing the last bridge. The Upper Spring is located at the bend in Carson's Loop.

The waters of these springs were supposed to have medicinal qualities, which I have been trying to ascertain. So far, my research has been sketchy.

According to the report of a visitor to Carson Springs in 1888, the Lower Spring was referred to as Lithia Spring. It was also called the Yellow Spring in Samuel Carson's 1816 grant. Medicinally, the waters of this spring were superior to that of the Upper Spring.

A lithia spring is one containing lithium oxide. However, folks still remember that this water had a high iron content, as evidenced by the rusty residue on the vessels in which it was collected. In some of his writings, Governor Ben. W. Hooper refers to the Upper Springs as the Chalybeate Spring, which by definition would indicate that it was impregnated with the salts of iron.

Others have written that this was a sulphur spring, but no one has mentioned the odor that usually accompanies sulphur water. The visitor to Carson in 1888, who had also visited there in 1848, gave this description of the Upper Spring: "The sulphur spring was the only thing I found unchanged. A gum made by sawing a hollow tree is placed in the spring, with the red and purple sediment of sulphur inside, might be the same I saw forty years ago."

Another visitor in 1888 had this to say about the Upper Spring: "A short distance from the Lithia spring, and up among the cottages, is the gum tree Sulphur spring. This water is also excellent, though the medicinal properties are said to be inferior."

Mrs. O'Dell wrote that the springs were thought to be good for ridding the body of malaria. In his writing about Carson Springs and the medicinal claims, Donald McSween said:

Whether these claims were justified is a somewhat moot question, but the fact that the waters—particularly those of the Lower Spring—were pleasant to the taste, excellent thirst quenchers, and somewhat addictive is indisputable. Those who had drunk these elixirs for any time found the water back home unpalatable and unsatisfying and many Newportans regularly made the trip...to fill up jugs, large bottles, fruit jars or other containers to take back

Upper Spring, 1912. *Courtesy of Beverly C. Little.*

Lower Spring, 1912. *Courtesy of Beverly C. Little.*

with them for drinking purposes. Homes where this practice was prevalent were easily identified for the glass containers would take on a distinctive reddish patina from the strong mineral content of the water.

McSween also wrote of having seen advertisements for Carson Springs listing all of the ailments for which the water was good, along with testimonials of those who had benefited.

Beth Runnion recalls that her grandmother only used water from the Lower Spring before dinner and water from the Upper Spring after dinner. Such reasoning was based upon the effects that the different waters had on the body.

In 1888, the visitor described the Lower Spring:

> *The spring has a beautiful marble basin with "Carson's Lythia Spring" engraved upon it, and a pretty latticed house with comfortable seats has been built over it, which I understand was the enterprise of Mr. Walter Carson. If bears no resemblance to the stage of rocks, which tradition says was formed by nature, but which it be more logical to suppose had been hewn by Indians.*

Judging from a photograph taken about 1912, the above-mentioned spring house was falling into disrepair. There is no record of how long it lasted, but about 1934, a new structure was built there. The following undated clipping was found in a scrapbook:

> *Work on Spring at Carsons*
> *The work that is being done on the spring at Carsons is nearing completion and it is going to be safe from contamination for ever as well as being attractive and inviting in appearance.*
> *Like all such undertakings it is costing more than expected and if people who enjoy driving out to Carsons to cool off and get a good drink will help a little, no one will be hurt...C.E. McNabb will gladly accept any amount you may care to give to this very worthy civic movement.*

L.W. (Tige) Hooper said that he and Mr. Samples did a lot of the construction work on the new gazebo over the Lower Spring. A concrete slab was poured, which elevated the spring water above the level of the creek. There was a depression about eighteen inches deep in the center of the slab. Down in the depression was a pipe from which the water flowed, and at the bottom was an opening that drained into the creek. A rock wall with seats surrounded three sides of the structure, which had a pointed roof and was latticed around the eaves. There was a plaque inscribed "Carson Springs 1816," which was the date of Samuel Carson's first grant.

This spring house remained until some time after 1971, when I think it burned down. The concrete base is still there, but the center depression is filled with mud and debris.

Today no one recalls a covering over the Upper Spring, but one of the photographs of the old Peterson Hotel indicates that there may have been a covering over it at one time. This spring was encircled with a wall of bricks and the water bubbled up in the center. The wall was constructed in such a way to keep dogs and cats from drinking at the spring source. The water then drained into a branch that ran down to the creek.

Some of the other news items about Carson Springs in 1888 appeared in the *Morristown Gazette*:

JULY 16, 1888:

> *Carson Springs has about one hundred and fifty visitors, most of whom are families occupying their own cottages. The Rodgers House, during the past two or three weeks, has had about twenty-five regular boarders. Of the one hundred and fifty persons now there two-thirds are seeking rest and health and the remainder pleasure and pastime.*
>
> *The water has a large per cent of iron and other minerals in it and is highly recommended for its curative and strengthening qualities…The highest the thermometer has registered at this place so far this summer is 87 degs. We have fires to sit by morning and night…*
>
> *Among the ladies who are camping here are the Misses Eckle, the Misses Susong, Miss Nannie Bee Robinson and friend Miss Tullis, of Nashville, Mrs. I.K. Franklin and sister Miss Kate Harrison…*
>
> *Hugh Goughenour, Will and Charlie Mims, and a number of other handsome young men from Newport attended the hop at the Rodgers House Tuesday night.*
>
> *Thursday last, five of us—Messrs. Holloway, Kite, Powers, Hooper and Helms—faced butte's mountain, at the steepest point in the neighborhood of the springs, and began its ascent. When about half way up we would all willingly have tried a descent; but pride and fear urged us forward until the summit was reached.*

JULY 18, 1888: "A 'grand mountain' excursion and hop is to take place today (Tuesday) at Carson Springs, near Newport. Dancing will begin at 8 o'clock p.m."
JULY 25, 1888: "Quite a number of whitewashed cottages had been built, conspicuous among which is that of Col. Moore its altitude giving it

every advantage over the rest…The mechanic's hammer was sounding vigorously, preparing residences for Col. John Stokely and Mr. A.R. Swann, of the Beaver Dams."

AUGUST 1, 1888:

> *J.M. Rodgers, proprietor of the Rodgers House, Carson Springs, was in the city Monday and made us a welcome call. He reports the cottages all filled and a good crowd at the Rodgers House. No more intelligent and well to do representatives of any counties of any State can be found at any mountain health resort than the Swans, Stokelys, Jacks, Moores, Taylors, Susongs, Robinsons, Dunns and many others who are now enjoying the delightful atmosphere and health-giving waters at Carson Spring with their families and servants.*

AUGUST 14, 1888:

> *After satisfying the cravings of the inner man we strolled about the little village until it was almost time for the nightly dance to commence at the Rodgers House…Soon the strains from old George's bow announced that everything was in readiness…*
>
> *The light fantastic was tripped until the wee small hours of the morning, and one and all united in saying that it was a most enjoyable occasion.*

APRIL 24, 1889:

> *Mr. W.P. Carson will sell at public auction, on May 11th, 34 lots at Carson Springs, near Newport. The lots will be sold with right to use water from the Lithia Spring. This is a good opportunity to secure cheap a lot for a summer camp at one of the most pleasant retreats in East Tennessee. Mr. W.H. Coffman of Morristown, will conduct the sale.*

PART III

For seventy-five years after the first lots were sold in 1885, Carson Springs was a haven for many people during the hot days of summer. Rustic cottages were constructed to house the families. Some of the cottages were more elaborate than others, but many of them were little more than weatherboarding nailed to framing, with a roof overhead, of course.

I am guessing that some of these houses in the first days probably did not even have window sashes; probably they only had shutters that opened from the bottom and were propped up with sticks. Window screens had not yet become popular.

Electricity and indoor plumbing were nonexistent. Drinking water was carried from either of the two springs, and all other water was taken from the creek. Outdoor privies were the norm. The W.D. McSween home, Bonnie Brae, was one of the first homes to have indoor plumbing, which was a gravity system from the creek. Electricity was furnished to the McSweens by their own Delco system, when it chose to generate.

As time passed, the cottages became more convenient. Electricity was available to the area in the early 1940s through the Rural Electrification Program. It has only been in recent years that residents there could have access to public water; most were dependant on wells. Telephone service was offered about 1950.

It was not the conveniences, however, that the summer residents sought. It was relief from the heat and the participation in the social community. There were individuals of all ages, so nearly every child would have a playmate. There were mountains to climb, woods to explore and the creek for swimming and playing.

At the head of Carson, probably on property that is now a part of the Camp Carson, was a swimming hole that had been created by damming the creek with a wooden dam. This dam eventually gave way or deteriorated to such an extent that the summer residents paid to replace it with a concrete one. It is recalled that Alf Taylor donated the concrete and many of the young men, like Tige Hooper and Charles Seehorn, did the actual work.

This swimming hole could accommodate a large number of bathers, and there was no admission charge to swim there. During the summer weekends, hordes of folks came out to swim. There were no dressing rooms, so people changed into bathing suits in their cars. There were no swimming pools at that time in Cocke County. The City Park pool was not constructed until about 1936. The first private pool, I think, would have been that of the W.B. Stokelys.

The following article was published in the *Newport Plain Talk* on July 27, 1911:

> *Many Visitors at the Springs*
> *Carson Springs is the Mecca for Newport people and every cottage has an occupant. The population of the old resort has increased now until it is well over 100 and more are coming daily. The lower spring has been put in fine shape and campers are having a good rest...*

Among those at the Springs are Mrs. Anna R. Stokely and family, Fred and Miss Eva Fisher, Mrs. George Gorrell, Rev. Mr. Free, Sheriff Allen and wife, Mrs. John M. and John Burnett Stokely, Zeb Clevenger and family, A.O.P Hill and daughters of Dandridge, J.R. Knisley and family of Wilsonville, Mrs. Sue Susong and family, the two Misses Haynes of Rock Cliffe, N.C., Robert Reese and family of Reedtown, Mr. And Mrs. J.W. O'Hara, Will Jack and family, Mr. and Mrs. J.R. Jones, Mrs. R.C. Smith, Mrs. John M. Jones, Miss Rowena Carson, and Mrs. Will Stokely and family.

On Sunday Newport was practically depopulated and every possible conveyance carried some of the people of this city to the Springs.

Sunday visitors could have been going to swim or to visit family and friends who were there for the summer. The hotel offered a Sunday dinner, and people still remember the delicious fare.

Some who operated the hotel in its latter days were the Swanson family, the Ted Roadman family and Mrs. Wade Giles.

Besides the porches, which most of the cottages had, folks could gather at the community common or park, which had been set aside for the use of visitors by Mrs. Sue E. Susong. (This site is still there and still supposedly belongs to no one person.)

Donald McSween wrote this about the park: "At one time it had a croquet court with seats around its perimeter, a gazebo, horseshoe pitching area, swings and other refinements for the enjoyment of both the cottage owners and hotel guests. Rights to this common area and to the waters of both springs were granted in perpetuity to those buying lots."

A glimpse into the summer social life of Carson Springs can be found in the following article, which was published in the *Newport Plain Talk*, September 4, 1913:

The season of social affairs at Carson Springs has closed. Many delightful affairs were held, the committee in charge being Mrs. J.R. Seehorn, Mrs. B.W. Hooper, and Mrs. Hugh Alexander.

A enjoyable farewell concert was given last Thursday evening, it being featured by a farewell address by Mr. Estes.

The program was as follows: Reading by Mrs. Seehorn which was highly appreciated, Mrs. Seehorn being a talented reader whose public appearances are always welcomed.

Mr. And Mrs. Alexander gave several vocal selections including Scotch songs. Mr. Alexander made quite a hit during the National Spanish song in Spanish.

A selection was rendered by a trio composed of Mr. and Mrs. Alexander and Mrs. Hooper. This was followed by a quartette rendered by Mrs. Hooper, Mrs. Purkey and Mr. and Mrs. Alexander.

Clog dancing by the celebrated artists, Mrs. Bardwell and Mrs. B.D. Jones followed.

Mesdames Estes, O'Hara, C.E. McNabb, and Miss Mae Stokely were also numbered on the program and deserve special mention as their parts were especially good.

The program was concluded by a farewell speech by Mr. G.W. Estes, which was greatly enjoyed.

During the program of the campers, Messrs. McNabb of Wilsonville and the Owenby boys rendered a number of selections on the banjo, guitar, and violin which added greatly to the occasion.

The above-mentioned swimming hole met with disaster during a cloud burst about 1933. Because the water side of the dam was perpendicular rather than slanted, it gave way to the onslaught of water. After that, Mrs. J.W. Kyker constructed a pool, which she named the Crystal Lake, on her property. Water for the pool was channeled in from the creek. A bathhouse was also built. This created a bit of bad feelings among the summer residents because Mrs. Kyker, of course, charged admission and the original swimming hole had been free. The Crystal Lake was still being used in the mid-1950s. The remains of the pool are still there, and the bathhouse is now a residence.

Another swimming hole was built on the creek about two miles below Carson Springs proper by R.H. Sexton. This was known as the Splash-A-Way, and was located just below the bridge on Splashaway Road. This spot had a pavilion and lights and featured dances, too. But it is not to be confused with an actual pool of the same name, which was constructed by O.L. Clark in the mid-1950s.

Many of the families who had cottages came and stayed the entire summer; some only stayed part of the time and rented them out at other times. Ownership of the cottages changed over the years.

Whereas the boys might go camping, the girls preferred the house parties at Carsons. Usually six or eight girls with a chaperone would take food and bedding and go to one of the cottages for a week or so. There was swimming and picnicking during the day, and at night there were usually boys who would stop by for visits. The end of the week probably found the girls exhausted because they had gotten little sleep with all of their late-night card games and talking.

Governor Ben W. Hooper said that about 1913 there was "a new crop of landowners by reason of sales of the old landowners and the sale of a new subdivision to another generation." The governor himself acquired quite a bit of acreage around both springs, some of which is still owned by his family. He loved Carson Springs, and in 1925 wrote articles in the *Newport Plain Talk* about it. He was desirous to see that a sanitation system was constructed, and also advocated that the road to be widened and the right of way cleared of boulders. He also addressed the fact that weekend visitors were littering the area with their picnic remains and the public order was sometimes violated by drunkenness, rowdiness and vandalism.

Part IV

Summer life at Carson Springs during its heyday would be considered primitive by today's standards. Most cottages had no electricity. There were no televisions, although there were a few battery-operated radios. Cooking was done on wood or oil stoves. Most homes did not have running water, so baths were generally taken through gravity with creek water, but they had only cold water. At times, the creek water was so cold that watermelons could be left in it for a time and get completely chilled.

The residents were on their own to provide their own modes of entertainment. As mentioned previously, there were lots of children, and children can usually find some way to amuse themselves, although not always in ways acceptable to parents.

One lady recalled that groups each summer usually hiked up English Mountain to the Signal Pole, part of a chestnut tree to which torches were attached during the Civil War to warn that the enemy was approaching. The wives, after their housework was done, visited with each other and often joined in games of bridge or rook. Some folks had hand-cranked Victrolas, which would provide music for singing and dances.

The road to Carsons was not paved until July 1950. The number of cars was limited, which meant that travel back and forth to town was also limited. Local businessmen of course came into town to work in the mornings and returned in the evenings. Anyone needing something from town had to catch a ride with one of them and wait around in town until one of them was returning. Usually those going to town also had a list of items to get for other residents. For several years in the 1920s and 1930s, Henry Alexander did operate a small grocery store just above the Lower Spring.

When the Great Depression struck, some families could not return to Carson Springs. They did not have enough money to maintain a cottage there and also one in town. The cottages stood empty or were rented. Right after the Depression came World War II, and there was little activity at Carson Springs during that time. For one thing, gasoline was rationed and it would have been difficult for the businessmen to have made the daily trips into town.

After the war, Carson Springs was revitalized. Modern conveniences arrived in the area. New cottages were built and older places were updated. While this new era was different in many ways than earlier times, there was a definite summer social community.

My family visited there many times, but, in the summer of 1958, we spent an entire week. There was so much for a kid to do. We walked up and down the road. We fished minnows using a fruit jar on a string, and when our jar broke Esther Hooper gave us another one. We swam in the creek and the Myers pool.

On several evenings, John Holder (wearing a beret that Grace Franklin had brought him from a trip to France) would load his Jeep with as many youngsters as were available and ride us up and down the road. One night we went over to Clevenger Town, where there was a watermelon slicing for some gubernatorial candidate. Those trips seem scary now when I think of that little Jeep and a bunch of wiggly kids. There could have been eight or ten on any given night.

Another milestone in the history of Carson Springs was the establishment of Camp Carson. Governor and Mrs. Hooper and Mrs. and Mrs. Charles Rhyne Sr. donated the property to the Tennessee Baptist Convention in 1949. Carl P. Daw was pastor of the First Baptist Church, and I heard him say at the church centennial that it must have been divine guidance that provided the success of this transaction between a Methodist Democrat and a Republican Baptist.

I have arbitrarily set 1960 as an approximate ending date for the summer community at Carson Springs. As I recall, that is about when a lot of the folks I knew stopped summering there. I cannot say precisely what brought about the change. Perhaps it was the availability of home air conditioning that made it unnecessary to go there to escape the heat; no doubt each family had its own reasons for not returning. Except for the campers, there are no summer residents at Carson Springs; those who remain live there all year.

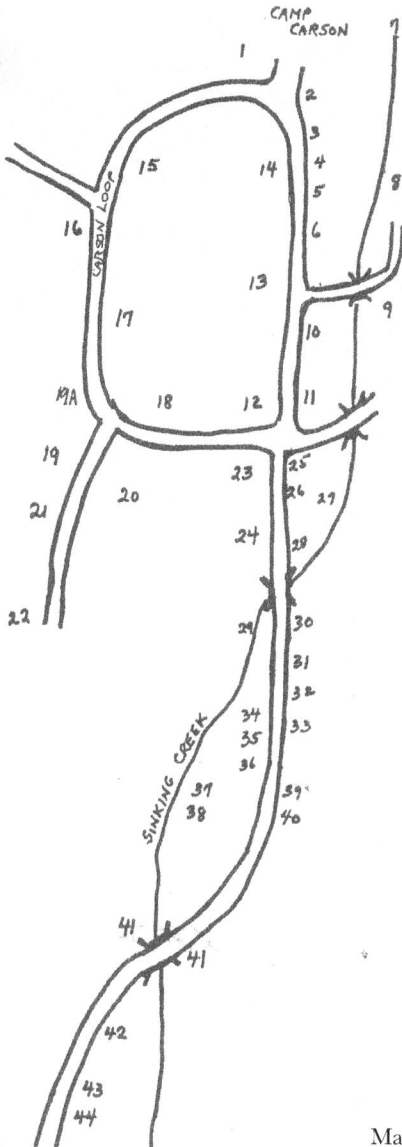

Map of cottages. *Author's collection.*

Based on my research, I have constructed a crude map showing the location of some of the cottages, basically between the years 1920 and 1960. I know that this will not include all the cottage sites or all the families who might have summered there. Over the years, some cottages were removed or burned and those living today have no recollection of them. I will also admit that I would not be successful as a cartographer.

Here is the listing of sites on the map.

1. E.L. Sellers/W.M. Crawford
2. Alwyn Kyker
3. Hugh Allen
4. Ned Doak
5. A.H. Taylor
6. Allen Kyker
7. Swimming hole
8. J.W. Kyker and Crystal Lake
9. W.D. McSween
10. Bruce Helm
11. Mrs. Dave Robinson/Connie Overholt
12. Dr. J.W. O'Hara/ Mrs. Kate Stokely
13. George F. Smith
14. Frank Taylor
15. _____Gorman
16. Charlie Clift
17. Jesse Fisher
18. John M. Jones/H.L.W. Taylor
19. Hotel
19A. Upper Spring
20. John Ownby
21. Fred Fisher
22. A.R. Swann
23. Community park
24. Croquet ground
25. J.L. Chilton/Ross Nichols
26. Henry Alexander
27. "The Shack" (operated by Juddy Huff)
28. J.R. Seehorn
29. Lower Spring
30. Ben W. Hooper
31. Mrs. Janie May Stokely
32. George Gorrell/Mrs. Emma Stokely
33. L.S. Smith/Fred Sharp
34. C.E. McNabb
35. Charles S. Runnion
36. Mrs. Grace Franklin
37. John Holder
38. John C. Holder
39. Winston Northcutt
40. McSween sisters
41. Fred L. Myers
42. Bill G. Williams
43. Sam Stanbery
44. Clyde Hodge

It is not difficult to see that Carson Springs has, indeed, changed over time. Even though Governor Hooper was both a lover of Carson Springs as well as a proponent of progress, he himself sounded a warning bell in an article in the *Plain Talk and Tribune* on September 20, 1950, nearly a half-century ago:

> *The coming of the camp, the building of phone lines, the installation of electricity and the construction of a new highway have all combined to revitalize Carson Springs. In fact there is some indication of a boom in land prices. This might or might not be a healthful condition. It is the sort of thing that has so often been overdone.*

The governor probably would not be pleased with parts of that area now, but Carson Springs as he knew it is a page from the past.

History of the High Oak Tulip Gardens

There was a time when thousands of folks from various parts of the United States looked forward to spring, when they could come to Newport to visit the High Oak Tulip Gardens of Mrs. Lillie E. Duncan. These gardens were on the grounds surrounding her home, which is now 281 North Street.

Mrs. Duncan was born Lillie E. Jones in 1875 in Greene County, near Warrensburg. She came to Newport in 1897 when she married George C. Duncan, one of the partners of Duncan and Greer Hardware (now Newport Hardware).

In 1919, when Lillie was only forty-four years old, she was diagnosed with an illness, possibly diabetes. The treatment prescribed outside exercise. It was then that she started to develop her property into formal gardens. Little by little, the gardens expanded to cover much of the ten-acre Duncan tract. She opened the gardens to the public in 1931, and for the next dozen or so years, crowds of people came here to view them.

A magazine article by Maude Weidner Jessen in 1937 had this description:

> Although it is known as the High Oak Tulip Garden, it belies its name in offering a wealth of blossoms from the first jasmine in January to gorgeous chrysanthemums in late November. And in December there are the lovely green shrubs and the evergreens, one of which—a native red cedar—"blossoms" out in colorful and gay Christmas decorations each Christmas Eve.

Entrance to High Oaks, home of Mrs. Duncan. *Courtesy of Asheville Post Card Co.*

However, as the name implies, it was during the tulip season that the gardens were the most spectacular. Starting with a single bed of tulips, Mrs. Duncan added more and more bulbs to her collections. One year she put out eight thousand bulbs. Some of the brand names were Darwin, Breeder and Cottage. Some of the bulbs were ordered directly from Holland.

Continuing with Mrs. Jessen's narrative:

> In the garden are some of the lovely yellow Darwin which was only recently developed, and the white Darwin, a fragile and beautiful variety. Some of the loveliest specimens in the garden are President Taft, a luscious dark red; Benjamin Franklin, another exquisite Darwin; Zwanenburg, a beautiful white tulip; and the Captain Lindbergh, a tulip which does justice to the name.
>
> Just to mention the names of these beautiful tulips in such a manner gives no idea of the way one feels when looking over an immense stretch of color so delightful and varied that it defies description—deep purplish black, very pale lavender, rich yellow and the most shimmering pale yellow, deep cream and a vivid white, white with a mere touch of pink—the Painted Lady—and many others for whose colors I can find no words in my vocabulary.

Driveway of High Oaks. *Courtesy of Asheville Post Card Co.*

Can you not let your imagination wander as you bring the palette of colors into your mind's eye?

All of this took lots of planning and execution. Charlie Brabson and Joe Jackson, full-time employees, did most of the heavy work, working year-round to maintain the gardens and the grounds. These men are recalled as large, strong individuals who did most of the work with shovels and wheelbarrows. Mrs. Duncan was often there with them to direct the planting. She also kept a garden book, a record of "planting, blooming, unusual plant development, orders placed and delivered, and of visitors to her garden."

Mrs. Jessen said,

> *Mrs. Duncan's generosity with her garden is repaid by her townsmen in their interest in High Oaks. Their interest takes the form of gifts of unusual plants for the garden...an odd piece of stone, a handful of fancy fish for the fancy fish pool or a rare fossil to decorate one of the many stone walls...Just to mention a few of the other places of interest in the garden, there is the fancy fish pool...the lily pool...the hanging rock garden...the spring and rock garden, where trillium, jack-in-the pulpits, bleeding heart, wild columbine and mint grow in profusion.*

High Oak Tulip Gardens. *Courtesy of Asheville Post Card Co.*

Depending on the weather, the gardens were opened during April, usually in the last couple of weeks. The *Newport Plain Talk* announced the openings each year and printed the rules. Visitors were asked to park on the street and allow the driveways to be reserved for the elderly and disabled. Visitors were asked not to touch or pluck the flowers, and children were to be accompanied by parents. It was also asked that children not play in the pools. Visitors were requested to stay only on the walkways.

In 1933, the Kiwanis Club helped with crowd control. Little girls dressed as butterflies acted as pages. The Newport Band, directed by Mike Crino, presented a concert one Sunday afternoon.

The next year, 1934, electric lights were strung so that the gardens could stay open until ten in the evening. The local businesses provided an entire page of advertising in the local paper, supporting Mrs. Duncan. Professor Alexander Lee, a Newport native, brought his band over from Johnson City. Other musical groups were presented, such as the Four Nightingales, an African American female quartet, and the Yellow Jackets, a local dance band. On one Saturday alone, 3,500 people visited the gardens.

For some reason, I could find no mention of the gardens in 1935, but in 1936 there were no lights, so the gardens were closed at 5:00 p.m. The Tanner Training School Sextet, the Gregg's Chapel Choir, the Brimer Quartet and the Cocke County High Mixed Quartet provided music.

In 1937, the Queen Esthers, a group of women from the Methodist Episcopal church, were in charge of the garden presentation. This was the first year there was an admission fee—twenty cents. Once again there were electric lights, so the gardens stayed open at night. The gardens were written up that year in *Gardens of the South, Esso Road Service Magazine* and *Holland's*.

The next year the Friendly Bible Class from the Methodist Episcopal South church acted as hostesses. My grandmother was in that class, and she recalled that they dressed in Dutch costumes. That year, Mrs. Duncan gave two scheduled talks on the planning and development of the gardens.

Unfortunately, the newspaper microfilm stops with 1938. It is uncertain just how long Mrs. Duncan continued to open her gardens to the public. Mrs. Walter Barker, who has lived across the street from the site since 1942, recalls that they were still being opened when she moved there. Eva Sexton seems to think that World War II brought an end to this event, as gas rationing cut down on unnecessary travel.

Besides her gardens, Mrs. Duncan was a successful businesswoman, managing farms and rental properties. She is remembered as a friendly, likeable, broad-minded individual who did much to help those in need. Following an illness of nearly a year, she died on December 25, 1952, but during the previous fall, she was taken outside to watch the planting of new bulbs, looking forward to another spring season.

The poet Keats said, "A thing of beauty is a joy forever." Mrs. Duncan's tulip gardens are no doubt still a joy for those who remember this page from the past.

Cocke County Celebrates the Folklore of Grace Moore

May 3 through 10 is National Music Week, and this column will again focus on a part of the musical history of Cocke County: Grace Moore, an operatic soprano and movie star more than fifty years ago. Grace Moore was from the Del Rio community, more precisely Harmony Grove. However, in her autobiography, *You're Only Human Once*, she names her birthplace as Slabtown, which was another name for Nough, where the post office was located.

Grace's mother, the former Tessie Stokely, had deep roots in Cocke County. Her father, William Russell Stokely, a Confederate soldier, was a grandson of Royal and Jane Huff Stokely, as well as Russell and Sarah Hays Jones, who were pioneers in that area. Tessie's mother, Emma Huff Stokely, was a daughter of Thomas and Judith Nichols Huff. Jane Huff and Thomas Huff were both children of a Revolutionary War soldier who received a land grant on the north side of the French Broad River, dated July 11, 1788. Royal Stokely was the son of another Revolutionary War soldier, Jehu Stokely, who settled the area about 1790. Through the Huff, Jones, Nichols and Stokely families, Grace has a complex web of kin in this county.

Grace's father, Colonel Richard L. Moore, was from Murphy, North Carolina. He came to Del Rio as a drummer (salesman), met his wife and went to business there. Mrs. Roy T. Campbell Sr., who knew

Colonel Moore from Murphy, told me about going to Chattanooga once with her sister to attend one of Grace's concerts. Mrs. Campbell and her sister called at the Moore home to visit with her friend, Colonel Moore, who welcomed them with the greeting, "Well, here's Peachtree!" which referred to a community in their native Cherokee County, North Carolina. They were in the living room when Grace arrived. Her father looked up and gave Grace only a passing greeting before returning to his guests to talk about their days in Murphy. Attorney Campbell says that his mother's aunt, Miss Bertha Mayfield, tutored Grace and her siblings in Jellico.

There is a state historical marker on Highway 107 commemorating Grace's birthplace. The marker states that she was born December 5, 1901, although Mrs. Harle Cole always maintained that Grace was older than that. Mrs. Cole said that she herself was born May 18, 1898, at Slabtown, and that Grace was about eight months younger. Mrs. Cole's mother, Sallie Sorrell Franks, and Grace's mother were friends. The night that Grace was born, Mrs. Franks was called to help out, but she could not go because her baby Ethel was sick.

Mrs. Cole's recollections can be validated by the 1900 census. I found the Moores living on Morgan Street in Knoxville, with the following information: "Richard L. Moore, Merchant, born 1875, North Carolina, wife Tessie, born 1880, Tennessee, and daughter Gracie, born December 1898."

Mrs. Cole also remembers being with Grace when she had returned to Del Rio during summers to visit her folks. Once Grace and Ethel were riding, just ambling along on their horses. Suddenly Grace flicked Ethel's horse with her crop and it took off with a start and nearly threw Ethel off.

Another time Mrs. Cole remembers a pretty pair of shoes that arrived in the mail for Grace. The shoes were a little too small, but Grace was working very hard to get them on to wear to a party that night at the J.H. Burnetts'. As she struggled she stated, "I'm going to wear them, damn it!" and she did!

Miss Mary Rowe Ruble also knew Grace. Miss Ruble's father, Dr. J.W. Ruble, had delivered Grace. Miss Ruble told about going with a group of Cocke County folks to Johnson City to hear Grace sing. Grace's mother was in the balcony, and when she saw the homefolks, she stood up and called out to all of them.

Mrs. Ruble's sister, Mrs. W.J. Shanks, was a close friend of Mrs. Moore's. When Grace was killed in 1947, her body was returned to Chattanooga

Grace Moore. *Courtesy of Jan B. Maddox.*

for burial. Mrs. Shanks went to Chattanooga for the funeral, which was on a Sunday afternoon at the First Baptist Church. When she arrived the day before, she was told that she'd never get a seat in the church. Mrs. Shanks attended the Sunday worship service and when it was over she just remained in the sanctuary. She wasn't alone for long, because the undertaker began bringing in all the flowers. The church was packed for the funeral, but Mrs. Shanks had a seat.

Mrs. Chattie Stokely Rainwater was a first cousin of Grace's mother. Her father, A. Jehu Stokely, was Grace's grandfather's half-brother. Grace and Chattie were near the same age. Once when they were little girls, they decided to exchange dresses when they were playing. Their play later involved climbing a tree and, while doing this, Chattie tore Grace's dress, which she said was much finer than her own. She was petrified about what would happen to her, but Grace's mother just laughed about it.

Mrs. Judith Huff Turner recalled a time when Grace came down to visit Judith's grandmother, Mrs. Jane Huff, who was her great-aunt. The

Huff home was near the intersection of Highway 70 and the Long Creek Road. Mrs. Huff asked Grace to sing before leaving, and she stood on the porch and sang "The End of a Perfect Day" by Carrie Jacobs-Bond. Miss Judith used to say, "I'm sure her voice filled the whole river valley!"

It may have been another occasion, but Miss Judith told of Grace wearing a large picture hat covered with pink roses. She said, "I tried not to covet it," but her sister, Elizabeth Justus, quipped, "I bet you did!"

My friend Mary Carmichael grew up in Chattanooga, not far from the Moore home. She and a little friend used to go and visit Mrs. Moore, who was then confined to a wheelchair. They used to love to be shown Grace's gorgeous dresses.

Mack Leibrock was in charge of the Post Exchange in Cannes, France, during World War II. One day Grace and her husband, Mr. Paera, came in to buy cigarettes. There on the counter was a copy of the *Newport Plain Talk*, which had arrived that day. Grace asked whose it was. She was then introduced to Mack, and they shared memories of Newport and Cocke County. Grace quipped, "Part of my money built the Winston Theater!" Mack also remembered that Grace had to buy the cigarettes; her husband couldn't because he wasn't an American citizen.

The fact that Grace Moore was born in Cocke County would in this day compare to Dolly Parton having been born in Sevier County, although Dolly stayed there longer than Grace stayed here. Grace's name still has a familiar ring here, but sadly the time is coming when the mention of her name will only bring the response, "Who's she?" as it does with such names as Alma Gluck, Mary Garden or Madame Schumann-Heink. Then the life of Grace Moore will truly be a page from the past.

Caravan of Celebrities
Made Their Way
through Newport

Americans find a special attraction with the rich and famous, and no doubt Newport was abuzz on August 27, 1918, when word got out that Thomas A. Edison, Henry Ford, Harvey Firestone and John Burroughs were in town.

These men were on their way to Fort Myers, Florida, where they all had vacation homes. They were camping along the way. Their caravan included fifteen men and six trucks and autos. Whenever they stopped for the night, Mr. Edison prepared a lighting system for their camp with his own batteries. Prior to coming through Newport, the group had spent the night outside Jonesboro on the Will Lee farm.

Fortunately, I have found an original newspaper clipping from the *Knoxville Journal and Tribune*, August 28, 1918, which reports their visit here:

> *Newport was honored at noon today for an hour by the presence of guests of world fame. Thos. A. Edison, Henry Ford, and John Burroughs were the distinguished members of the party. The party seemed to be conducted by H.S. Firestone, manufacturer of the Firestone auto tires, of Akron, Ohio. The party was met a mile out of town by Governor Hooper and Mayor L.S. Allen.*
>
> *The party arrived at 11:45 o'clock and lunched at Mims hotel. After lunch the guests visited for a half hour, meeting and shaking hands with more than one hundred people who had gathered to see the distinguished visitors. Lieutenant Everett Greer on being introduced to Mr. Ford, stated*

Mims Hotel, which burned in 1951, was on the present site of the Newport City Hall. *Courtesy of Sally M. Burnett.*

to the latter that he had just left Michigan and reminded Mr. Ford that a state primary was being held there today in which he is running for United States Senator…A great many children came to meet Mr. Burroughs, whose books they have been reading in their nature studies in school. The noted author stated to them that he is still writing books, having three now in course of preparation for the press.

The party left at one o'clock over the Dixie highway for Asheville.

It was the most distinguished party of national figures that Newport ever had the honor of having as guests even for a brief period of time.

Also, I found another clipping, an article entitled "Seen and Heard" by J.S. Dunn, which I think came from a Knoxville newspaper. This article was quoting an article from the *Newport Optimist* written shortly after the death of Edison in 1931. According to this article, Governor Hooper and Mr. Allen started to Oldtown as a "reception committee" and planned to meet the party at the bridge. The caravan had already crossed the bridge and was pulled over to the side of the road "with a puncture in one of Mr. Firestone's famous tires." They had not planned to stop in Newport, but as they had been delayed by the puncture, they accepted the invitation to have their dinner meal at the Mims Hotel as the guests of Mrs. Mims.

The article continued:

Quickly the news of the coming of the celebrities spread throughout the countryside and with the spreading a crowd of citizens gathered to get a

Left: Thomas A. Edison. *Courtesy of the Burnett Smith Collection.*

Right: Henry Ford. *Courtesy of the Burnett Smith Collection.*

glimpse or clasp a hand of either or several of America's most renowned personages.

Thomas Edison, it is recalled, was somewhat weary when arriving here, and after shaking hands with a great number of citizens retired to his room in the hotel. Ford, Burroughs, and Firestone were more talkative...

Mrs. W.B. Robinson, who is a great naturalist and who was very familiar with the works of Burroughs, engaged in conversation with him talking about his books and other things that naturalists have in common. Other people made gestures and talked with Henry Ford about his product, he learning during the conversation that his newest product, the tractor, was in use by Stokely Bros. on a farm here. Firestone also met many people and revealed many interesting things into his private make-up.

After having been contacted about this visit in 1986 by Charles Gunter of Johnson City, who was doing research on this trip, I talked with Mrs. Myra Murray, whose parents operated the Mims Hotel. Mrs. Murray said that she always helped in the kitchen of the hotel and she remembered the day that these men were there for dinner, but she couldn't recall what was served that particular day. It could have been country ham, fried chicken or steak and gravy. The hotel meals were served "family style" at long tables. Guests just ate what was prepared that day; there was no ordering from a menu.

With the famous group was a photographer who made pictures during the trip. The Firestone Company sent the Mims family a picture of the group in front of the hotel, but Mrs. Murray said that it had been lost. Jim Franks said that Alf Mims once showed the picture to him. The Firestone Archives in Akron still has all of the pictures, but unfortunately they are not identified. Someone would have to go there and personally examine them in order to identify those from Newport.

My grandfather, who was an early Ford dealer, did have a small book about these men on a camping trip, but like the picture sent to the Mims family, it too has disappeared.

Recently in the Smith family pictures, two snapshots have turned up. They are not the best quality, but they are identifiable as Ford and Edison.

Thomas Alva Edison (1847–1931) has been called the greatest inventor in history. Everyone knows that he invented the electric light bulb and the phonograph, but many may not know that his genius improved the telephone, the typewriter, the motion picture and the electric generator. (I wonder if Edison retired from the crowd in Newport because he was deaf and conversation in a crowd would have been difficult.)

Henry Ford (1863–1945) manufactured his first automobile in 1896. With the development of the assembly line, Ford could mass-produce automobiles at a lower cost, making them more affordable to the general public. He also initiated profit sharing, the eight-hour workday and the grand daily wage of five dollars.

Harvey S. Firestone (1868–1938) pioneered in the field of automobile tires, which were first solid rubber, and then air filled. By 1927, Firestone, Ford and Edison were working together to develop a substitute for natural rubber.

John Burroughs (1837–1921) became a disciple of the writings of Ralph Waldo Emerson, Henry David Thoreau and Walt Whitman. He left his job in the professional world and became a naturalist. He was noted for his vivid descriptions of flowers, bees and birds.

Governor Hooper was quoted as having said that these men were "the most noteworthy group of celebrities to ever visit Newport." They certainly made a page in Newport's past.

Visit us at
www.historypress.net